# STILL LOVING TO MULLINIX

## A BREATHTAKING JOURNEY

Dear Connie,
Thank you and your family for walking part of this "breathtaking Journey" with me. It has been a joy knowing and loving you. May God's peace and presence go with you as you continue the journey.

Love & Joy,
Jerry Haywood
October 13, 2021

# JERRY HAYWOOD

© 2021

Published in the United States by Nurturing Faith, Macon, GA.
Nurturing Faith is a book imprint of Good Faith Media (goodfaithmedia.org).
Library of Congress Cataloging-in-Publication Data is available.

ISBN: 978-1-63528-143-9

Scriptures are taken from the NEW INTERNATIONAL VERSION (NIV): Scripture taken
from THE HOLY BIBLE, NEW INTERNATIONAL VERSION ®. Copyright© 1973,
1978, 1984, 2011 by Biblica, Inc.™. Used by permission of Zondervan.

Scriptures marked KJV are taken from the KING JAMES VERSION (KJV):
KING JAMES VERSION, public domain

Illustrations (cover and interior) by Clara Jebson.

# Many thanks to...

Clara "Mimi" Jebson, who captures the heart of these stories
with her gifted artistic illustrations

Candace Legere for her technical expertise and hours of labor
in preparing this manuscript for the publisher

My wife, Jean, who "loves" everything I write and constantly pushes
me to quit rewriting and call it finished

To the Walnut Hills church family, who shared their lives with me
and with whom I grew up in the faith

To all those readers of my first book, *Going to Mullinix*,
who encouraged me to write another book

To all those individuals whose lives have enriched my life
with reflections of God's presence and love

# Contents

# Preface: And So It Continues

There wasn't much to do in my hometown of Mt. Gilead, North Carolina, when I was growing up. Mostly we were dependent on our imaginations. Usually that was more than enough.

I read somewhere about a man saying his hometown was so small that "temptations were harder to find than resist." It wasn't quite that bad for us, but the one theater—creatively named the Gilmont—closed in 1954 when I was fourteen years old. That sad day marked the end of our places of entertainment.

But, like I said, we had our imaginations, so on Friday or Saturday night—and sometimes both—when there were no football or basketball games, my good friends, Wayne Dunn and David Warner, and our young basketball coach/teacher James Walton and I would pile into Walton's 1953 dark green Dodge sedan. Occasionally we would ride in Wayne's white 1952 Chevy.

Our conversation was always the same. "Well, where are we going tonight?" was always met with "I don't know" and "I don't care." So the familiar response would follow: "Okay, we'll just start out and see where the road takes us."

Back in the late 1950s, that was cheap entertainment since gasoline averaged around fifteen cents a gallon. When service stations engaged in a gas war, the price would drop even lower—sometimes into single digits.

Since our journey had no planned destination, we would sometimes end up in a strange town, searching for a sign telling us where we were. But that only added another dimension to our adventure. If you don't care where you are going, any road is okay, and any destination will do. If you care where your journey ends, however, the roads you choose to travel are crucial.

My first book, *Going to Mullinix*, grew out of my Pa-Pa's reply when anyone called out, "Where're you goin', Arthur?" Pa-Pa's answer was always a cheerful, "Goin' to Mullinix," followed by his signature big laugh.

Pa-Pa was my maternal grandfather with whom I shared the cab of a 1950 green Ford pickup as we made farm trips delivering chickens and chicken feed and then transporting the resulting eggs and fryers to processing plants in Rockingham or Hamlet. Most of that took place in the years between my tenth and twelfth birthdays.

Pa-Pa never told me where Mullinix was located, so it became, in my imagination, that mysterious safe place where everything fit and life was as it should be. Later, when I became a pastor, I almost subconsciously adapted Mullinix as a metaphor for that place of maximum kingdom living in which I take on the likeness of Christ to the degree my fallible discipleship is capable.

So Mullinix is not heaven. It is as close as I can get to *heavenly* citizenship while still living as a citizen of this world.

I told stories in that first volume of people, critters, and events, which I called "signs," giving direction to my journey. A pilgrimage like this is a step-by-step process and a lifelong challenge. Disappointment, discouragement, and failure hide around every curve, lurk in every valley, and poise atop every mountain.

Therefore, in this book, I tell the stories of a new collection of people, critters, and events that have "put heart back into me." Sometimes these "signs" were gentle nudges easy to miss unless I carefully exercised the "discipline of noticing." At other times they were dramatic, unmistakable road markers along the journey toward the "full stature of Christ." All of them together, however, revealed God's presence in such a way that it took my breath away.

So, with bated breath, the journey to Mullinix continues.

# Part One

A Breathtaking Journey

Has a Beginning

# An Unguided Vessel?

M y relaxing day of recreational fishing took a startling turn when my captain/
hostess suddenly grabbed the lines controlling the sails and cried, "I'm not sure
how to do this!"

It had been a delightful, sun-filled day on a quiet creek somewhere along the
Chesapeake Bay when dark clouds suddenly hid the sun and stiff breezes began to jerk
our boat in erratic directions.

One of my wife's friends, whom I'll call Jan, had learned of my love for relaxed
fishing (with the emphasis on *relaxed*). On three occasions I had experienced hard-driv-
ing deep-sea fishing adventures with the boat's crew baiting the hook and then setting

it before handing it to me while I spent the next hour struggling to pull the fish toward the boat.

Then, when it was close enough, the boat's crew took over again, brutally gaffing the beautiful fish aboard, flooding the previously scrubbed deck with bright red blood gushing from the open wound of the huge, flopping denizen of the deep, which had finally surrendered after a valiant fight for survival.

I quickly discovered that was not my idea of a good time. This was more like it: still water, warm sun in my face, beautiful landscape along the creek banks— a tranquil scene gently interrupted now and then by a passing fish, which I pulled in to admire briefly before dropping him or her back into the water to bite another lazy fisherman's hook.

Now, however, the day was taking a drastic turn. A distinct ring of panic in my hostess's voice turned rapt enjoyment into anxious concern as quickly as the weather had turned.

"I think we've run out of gas," Jan said excitedly. The motor, which had been propelling us quietly through the still water for several hours, now unexpectedly refused to start. However, I wasn't overly concerned as I looked up at the large sails. They were certainly capable of bringing us safely to shore.

But my confidence was mercilessly shattered when Jan exclaimed, "I'm not sure how to do this. My husband and son usually operate the sails."

That was not good news because neither her son nor her husband was within a hundred miles, and I was totally ignorant of the fine art of sailing. I had carefully relayed that bit of critical information to Jan when she made the initial invitation for me to join her on a fishing trip. Evidently she had not taken me seriously or perhaps felt there would be no need for any sailing acumen on my part.

Obviously she had been wrong. "I'm willing to help if you'll tell me what to do," I called out as she tried to untangle the lines and shift the sails so they would angle us toward the dock— approximately 200 yards in the distance.

"I have no idea what to tell you to do," she cried helplessly. The dock might as well have been 200 miles away as our boat continued to lurch left and right on a zigzag course.

But I was infinitely grateful to see that the shifting winds were sending us into a peaceful little cove—that is, peaceful until we arrived—where half a dozen abandoned boats lay mournfully rusting at anchor. My prayers of thanksgiving intensified greatly when it became obvious that if the winds had sent us in the other direction, we would have been floundering in the wide expanse of the now churning Chesapeake Bay, where we most likely would have never been heard from again.

"Look out!" I called helpfully as the bow of our boat—I think it was the bow— angled directly toward one of the boats, which, if its stage of deterioration was any indication, had been assigned to the graveyard years before. Remarkably, we glanced off the stern of the boat's carcass at an angle that lined us up perfectly for a collision with the next homeless boat.

For the next several extremely long minutes, we careened off one boat after another at various angles while we frantically grabbed on to anything stable to keep from falling overboard.

Looking up quickly as we banged off the hull of another boat, I marveled to see that we had miraculously pinballed off the decaying boats in such a way that we were inching closer and closer to the dock. *Inching* is the key word, as we would gain six feet and then lose three.

Momentarily taking my eyes off the next boat our mostly self-controlled vessel was targeting, I saw several men standing on the creekbank near the dock.

Well, for the time being they were standing. They looked in danger of tipping over at any moment from spasms of uncontrolled laughter. Some were holding their ample stomachs with both arms while others clutched their caps while scratching their heads in amazement at this bizarre game of "bumper boats" playing out before their eyes.

With a fresh burst of hope, even while almost losing my grip on my sanity along with the side of the boat, I noticed that we were continuing to make our uncertain way nearer and nearer the dock. One of the men, thankfully, restrained his hilarity long enough to go to the end of the dock, preparing to catch the land line he optimistically assumed I would be tossing to him.

Twice I heaved the rope as forcefully as I could, but each time it landed just short of the dock. Jan had been unable to slow the boat sufficiently as we swiftly sailed on by. The swirling wind also didn't help with my throwing accuracy.

Finally, by God's infinite grace, as we passed the dock for the third time, our rescuer controlled his amusement long enough to grasp the rope I had finally succeeded in tossing onto the end of the dock.

After our laughing hero had firmly secured us to the dock in spite of almost being jerked into the water, Jan thanked him profusely before turning to me and apologizing for bringing us to such a level of ridicule and danger. I told her that over many years I had grown comfortable enough with myself that the *danger* bothered me far more than the *ridicule*.

One of the most helpful advantages of growing older is that I care less and less about appearances and people's evaluations of those appearances. Besides, I long ago recognized how ridiculous I can be, so ridicule no longer possesses the power to seriously damage my self-image.

Gratefully planting my feet on firm ground—or, more literally, the firm wood of the dock— I told Jan not to worry about it. "In fact," I said with a chuckle, "what we've just survived is pretty much the way I've experienced much of life."

*Still Going to Mullinix*

"Oh no," Jan muttered under her breath as her body shook with a slight shiver. "What's wrong?" I asked.

"Nothing," she replied with a shrug as she continued to remove items from the boat. "I just felt the chill of a sermon coming on."

"No sermon," I replied laughing. "Just a few random thoughts." Jan just shook her head in resignation.

So later, as she drove us home, I told Jan that finding my way in this crazy world often seemed to take a frustrating, circuitous route, bouncing off one thing after another, one person after another, one event after another, one choice after another—sometimes at such an angle that I was heading toward my goal, but at other times sending me completely off course.

"Unexpected storms and shifting winds don't help either," I added ruefully.

Jan saw I was just getting warmed up and kept silent. So I continued, "But, guided by an unseen hand, each encounter miraculously has served to contribute toward my reaching the desired destination—if not mine, at least God's."

Jan remained silent and I took that as a sign she hadn't completely tuned me out. So I guess I've bought into the assurance that "And we know that in all things God works for the good of those who love him, who have been called according to his purpose" (Rom 8:28).

During this monologue, Jan had been quietly studying the road ahead as it grew increasingly darker. Finally, she shook her head and said, "Jerry, I know I don't show up at church very often. Christmas mostly. Every other year. Always liked Christmas with all the candles and carols. But I'm beginning to think I don't need to attend at all."

"What do you mean?" I asked.

"Well," Jan replied, with a deep-throated chuckle, "every time we're together, you sneak in a sermon somewhere along the way. Why waste my time with church when I'll bump into you somewhere and get the same thing?" She laughed softly at her jab but sounded serious. So I resigned myself to her absence from the church door for another five years or so.

"Well, you always seem to ask for it," I retorted. "What with all your questions." She didn't answer, so I added, "Actually, I *have* been thinking there might be a sermon in there somewhere—or maybe even a book."

"I knew it!" Jan exclaimed triumphantly. Still studying the road carefully, she finally asked, "What do you think might be the title—although your sermon titles never seem to have anything to do with what you actually say." She never gave me a break.

Not giving her the pleasure of acknowledging her latest jab, I thought for a few moments before adding, "I don't know. What do you think of *A Breathtaking Journey?*"

Jan was silent for a few moments before asking, "You mean like you stopped breathing each time we collided with another boat?"

"Well, that's part of it," I chuckled. "But I was really thinking about how breathtaking it is that we finally reached the dock in spite of all our ignorance and mistakes along the way."

"Now wait a minute!" Jan protested. "Who are you calling ignorant?"

"That's not a description of your personhood," I replied quickly. "In fact, I've always thought you were rather intelligent." A small, satisfied smile appeared briefly on Jan's face. "But you confessed that you didn't know anything about controlling the direction of the boat with the sails. That's the ignorant part I was talking about. And it was quite obvious," I added with a sly smile.

"That's true," Jan conceded reluctantly. "But we did make it to the dock."

"That's what I'm talking about!" I said. "That's the *real* breathtaking part of it—that we actually reached our destination in spite of all the bouncing off boats and shifting winds and minimal help from us."

I didn't want to push it. It *was* becoming dangerously close to a full-blown sermon. So I was quiet for the rest of the trip, staring out at the driving rain, almost hypnotized by the little white droplets bouncing off the black asphalt, trying to obscure the shimmering center line intended to guide us home.

Forty minutes later, Jan dropped me at the church parking lot where I had left my car. After thanking her for the day—in spite of all our misadventures—I made the short drive home safely through the still-raging storm. I called Jan a few minutes later to make sure she had also arrived home.

I was still amazed that we had made it.

Crawling into bed an hour later, the thought struck me: "With God's help—in spite of all the obstacles—I guess reaching Mullinix *is* a possibility. Maybe attaining authentic Christlikeness does not have to remain merely a distant dream."

I was finding it difficult to breathe at the very wonder of it all. Pulling the covers up to my chin, I forced myself to resume a slow, rhythmic breathing.

A few minutes later, I fell into a peaceful sleep.

# Faith and Jumping Out
# of Airplanes

I have never liked surprises—especially at 2:30 in the morning. During my years as a pastor, those early morning calls always meant bad news.

But there it was, a 176-pound surprise landing on top of me with a bloodcurdling scream as two muscular arms encircled me in a viselike grip at exactly 2:30 a.m. "Gotcha this time!" the sinister voice exclaimed in triumph.

My time in Williamsburg seemed to be over before it had begun.

"You did what?" I exclaimed much louder than I had intended. But I was astounded—and deeply impressed. Sue Yeatts had casually informed me while we were standing in line for food at our weekly Wednesday night church supper at Walnut Hills that she had jumped out of a plane to mark her seventy-second birthday.

Sue and her husband, Andy, are longtime friends and, since they joined our family of faith in the mid-eighties, have been very much a part of our varied ministries. Each has held multiple positions of leadership in addition to providing us with many laughs. Andy always has a joke and a smile.

One of my favorites is when Andy was asked if he knew Virginia Albrecht, a special lady who was always baking for anyone who looked hungry or whom she loved. She loved everyone. Sadly, Virginia recently fell and broke her hip at ninety-nine years of age and died quietly the next morning prior to surgery.

A couple years prior, someone asked Andy if he knew Virginia. Andy quickly replied, "Oh, yes, I've known Virginia for twenty pounds." That perfectly described my own experience.

But, like I said, Andy and Sue are valuable members of our church. Much too valuable for Sue to be disembarking from an airplane before it lands.

"How could you do that, Sue?" I asked incredulously. Not only did the act itself seem frightening, but Sue had told me earlier that she was a "control freak." I'm not sure I've reached "freak" status, but I am definitely disfigured in the "control" direction. I have enough trouble just getting on a plane and placing my life under the control of a total stranger.

"I just don't understand, Sue," I continued. "How could you leave the solid footing of a perfectly good airplane and fling yourself into empty space, gripped in the arms of a complete stranger?"

"Wait a minute," she laughed. "He wasn't a *complete* stranger. I had carefully researched his company and his personal record. The only accident they've had was a broken ankle by one of their clients. I could get a broken ankle walking through my front door."

"So you had a lot of faith in him, huh?" I said.

"Complete faith," Sue replied, nodding her head emphatically. "I wasn't nervous in the least."

I was still greatly intrigued by the whole thing as I reached for my meal, even though a sudden knot in my stomach had mostly destroyed my appetite. Looking over my left shoulder, I continued my questioning: "How did he do it—count 'one, two, three, JUMP'?"

"No," Sue replied casually, picking up her plate of tasty cordon bleu prepared by the expert hands of Jerry Simmons. "We just walked over, sat in the doorway, and slid off."

Even though I love cordon bleu—especially the way Jerry prepares it—the visual Sue had just thrust into my mind left me slightly nauseated (probably the broccoli served along with the cordon bleu also had something to do with it).

Through the years I often visited church members in the hospital right after lunch. Invariably, as we were talking, a cafeteria employee would pop in to collect the food tray. Ninety-nine times out of a hundred, the food tray collector would lift the plate covering to see if the patient had eaten.

The hallways were already permeated with the pungent aroma of broccoli—obviously the favorite food of hospitals everywhere. But when the plate lid was lifted, a powerful odor of leftover broccoli now wilted into sickly limpness would fill the room. Mix that with all the traditional medicinal smells of hospitals—well, maybe you can understand why I have developed a strong aversion to broccoli (forgive me, mothers everywhere).

But I digress.

Sue was off to her usual table of friends but called over her shoulder, "You really should consider doing it on your next birthday, Jerry," she said cheerfully.

"Never!" I called out as I held my fork and knife poised to cut into the cordon bleu as soon as my temporary nausea passed. "I could never give up control like that."

But as I ate in silence, ignoring the conversations around me, I thought, "Wait, maybe I have. Maybe I have found the courage—or rather the faith—to jump out of an airplane."

Surprised at that sudden realization, I remembered my first foray into the little village of Williamsburg, Virginia, back in 1969 and that body landing on top of me out of the dense darkness.

I had arrived two hours earlier on the day before I was to preach a "trial" sermon at Walnut Hills Baptist Church. At that time there was no actual church building. Rather, a handful of determined people were meeting in Rawls Byrd Elementary

School cafeteria—later renamed Laurel Lane Elementary School. It seems a character flaw had been discovered in the man for whom it was originally named and so the name had to be changed. There are advantages of failing to be prominent enough to have even a closet named after you. Think of the embarrassment my progeny will be spared if years later the name of my memorial closet had to be changed because someone discovered an unexpected skeleton in one of its dark corners.

But back to my story. As the result of a miscommunication between myself and the chairman of the search committee, Norman Cullum, who later became one of my closest friends, the committee thought I was driving in early Sunday morning. This was long before cellphones, and when I found a payphone (ask your grandparents), I still could not reach him at the only number I had.

So I had stopped off to see a young man who had been a member of my youth group at Columbia Baptist Church in Falls Church, Virginia, where I was still serving. Greg Cooley was now a student at the College of William & Mary.

As it happened, Greg's roommate was out of town for the weekend, so Greg invited me to spend the night with him. Thus, I found myself nestled in a narrow dorm bed, struggling to sleep while filled with the anxiety of the next day—my first ever "trial sermon." The name itself was enough to bring tremors to a twenty-eight-year-old minister who had never been a pastor.

So imagine my surprise when I was ferociously attacked by a dark figure during the early morning hours in a supposedly safe dormitory room at such a prestigious institute of higher learning as the College of William & Mary.

In the next few minutes of hilarious explanation, however, I discovered that Greg's roommate and this friend—a pimply-faced freshman from down the hall—were in the middle of a game copied from the *Pink Panther* series so popular at the time.

Some of you will remember the interaction between Inspector Jacques Clouseau and his manservant, Cato Fong, a martial arts expert. Cato was instructed to attack Clouseau at unsuspecting times in order to keep the inspector's reactions sharp. The student from down the hall was obviously playing the role of Cato, and in this instance I was, unfortunately and unwittingly, Inspector Clouseau.

After a careful examination determined that I did not appear to have any permanent injuries, Greg could no longer contain his amusement, laughing uncontrollably for the next thirty minutes. "You sh-sh-should have s-s-seen your face when I turned on the l-light," he stammered between spasms of laughter while collapsing on his bed.

After we had turned out the lights an hour later and the mortified freshman had returned to his room, I was awakened from a restless sleep all during the night by spontaneous bursts of laughter from Greg's bed.

I didn't know it at the time, but those events were an omen of a weekend that for many reasons did not live up to any of our expectations. But that's another story.

The next day in the late afternoon, I was returning in record time to our home in Falls Church, where I informed my wife that, sadly, we would not see Williamsburg again except maybe as tourists.

But while I was composing my letter of regret to be mailed the next day, Dr. Curtis O'Shell, a deacon and professor at W&M, whose wife Marge was on the search committee, called and said that because of the weather—cold and snowy—many of the church leaders were unable to get back into town and wanted to set up an informal visit in the parsonage with all the church people.

At first thought, this was another disappointment because my decision and the church's decision had, up to this point, been easy—"No!" Now a complication had been inserted into my certainty of God's will. It's always frustrating when my conviction that I absolutely know what God wants takes an unexpected turn toward ambiguity.

After a conversation with my wife (Jean can be very persuasive—as many of you who absolutely refused to be in her plays suddenly found yourself in the lead role can testify), I reluctantly returned Curt's call and said we were open for a visit.

As history demonstrates, we fell in love with each other and were blessed beyond all our deserving that the love affair between our family and the church family was strong enough for those generous folks to allow me to remain as their pastor for thirty-five years.

So when Sue said, "You need to try it, Jerry," I replied, "Never." Then I realized I had taken that leap before—a leap into the unknown with the only certainty being an absolute trust in the One who holds all landings in his hands.

Through the years, I have used the phrase "leap of faith," attributed to the German theologian Søren Kierkegaard, many times in my sermons. But one year I researched this phrase more closely and discovered from several sources that "leap of faith" wasn't exactly what Kierkegaard had said.

A number of commentators are in agreement that a better interpretation of the phrase is a "leap *to* faith." That changes things quite a bit. The implication of the phrase "leap of faith" is a leap into a bleak, dark unknown. A "leap *to* faith," on the other hand, is more like a leap into a future that may not be clear but that we can trust because of our past experience of finding God trustworthy: "By faith Abraham, when called to go to a place he would later receive as his inheritance, obeyed and went, even though he did not know where he was going" (Heb 11:8).

So on that day in May 1969, I could leave a secure staff position in a prosperous church. I could take a reduction in salary. I could join my story with the story of a family of faith that had no permanent home. I could do that—even though I confess to a lot of fear and trembling—with no other assurance than trust in a God whom I had found faithful in the past. Somehow, I believed he would provide a safe landing for my family, which already included two small children.

Of course, that faithful group of believers calling themselves Walnut Hills Baptist Church made that same "leap to faith." They entrusted their leadership—even the construction of a church building—into the hands of an inexperienced young man who, on that first Sunday, was mistaken by the choir director to be one of their college students.

On her way out that Wednesday evening, Sue called out again, "You really do need to plan on jumping out of a plane on your next birthday, Jerry. It'll take your breath away."

This time, I smiled back and said, "I think I already have, Sue."

# The O.K. Corral on Strawberry Plains

"Pastor, I don't think we're going to settle our differences in here. Why don't we go out back of the church and see if we can work things out?"

The invitation came from a red-faced layman who often disagreed vehemently with Pastor Edgar Burkholder. The pastor, weary from all the fighting, put his arm over the man's shoulders, which were trembling with fury, and said quietly, "Friend, I don't think I can accept that invitation."

But Rev. Burkholder had accepted the invitation to become pastor of the little mission on Strawberry Plains Road in April 1964. He entered this particular ministry with some misgivings because he sensed that the view of what church was all about by a small but powerful minority differed from his own—and most church members'—understanding of church.

His fears were borne out as the pastor's four years of devoted ministry were filled with turmoil and conflict even though they were productive in drawing people to the little mission. Folks show up when a man loves God and loves people the way Ed Burkholder did.

But in 1968, on the advice of his doctor, who feared the stress was going to kill him, Rev. Burkholder resigned.

After a conversation with Burkholder prior to the fiftieth anniversary of the church, Tony Neal, the pastor who followed me at Walnut Hills, quoted that first embattled pastor as characterizing his experiences in Williamsburg in the mid-1960s as being "much like life in the Old West."

When I read that quote in the fiftieth anniversary booklet, the title for an essay popped into my mind—"The O.K. Corral on Strawberry Plains." Not only did I enjoy reading about the Old West, but I had also heard—multiple times—all the battles of the early years of the mission on Strawberry Plains Road.

The Rev. George Kissinger, director of the Peninsula Baptist Association, stepped in after Edgar Burkholder's resignation and advised the church to split into two congregations. Subsequently, about forty people left the mission and established residency in the Rawls Byrd Elementary School cafeteria. This is the group that called me as pastor on May 1, 1969.

I recently visited John Bazacos, one of those early leaders, on his eighty-eighth birthday. Due to a severe back problem, John had to move from his home into an assisted living facility.

As the vice president of a local bank, John was a valuable resource to the young church—particularly in financial matters. For instance, John's assistance was crucial in helping the church secure seed money for beginning construction of the first small building on Jamestown Road.

John and I had a great visit, reminiscing and retelling stories we had both heard and told many times before. The good thing about distance and the passing of time is that perspective changes and things that once were severe challenges and threats can even take on a certain humor.

John and I remembered not only how the invitation to "settle things out back of the church" was reminiscent of the Old West. Even the move to Rawls Byrd—now Laurel Lane school—had its battles.

On this particular Saturday, the move of half the resources to the new location was limited to one pickup. Consequently, the move required a long, tiring day of labor. So as the day drew to a close, folks kept dropping out to do other things until the workforce was down to John and another strong early church leader, Norman Cullum.

John settled back in his easy chair by the window of his room in the assisted living facility, which overlooked an attractive flower bed. I sat in his wheelchair as he recited once again the concluding chapter of moving day: "Norman and I thought we were finished when we suddenly realized that we were short by several hymn books for our first service in the school." Chuckling, John continued, "But while we were making our last load to Rawls Byrd, someone locked the screen door to the little mission building."

The memories were flowing rapidly now. "But like most screen doors in those days, a little piece of the screen above the hook latch had been peeled back."

Suppressing his laughter, John said, "So Norman reached in and lifted the little hook, and we walked in to retrieve seventeen more hymn books—the number we knew belonged to us."

John paused again as he chuckled quietly. "Later that night, I was reclining in my easy chair at home, tired from the day's move, when a knock came at the door." John readjusted his position in the big chair as he looked at me with clear, amused eyes.

"Standing in the porch light was a deputy sheriff who had been a friend of mine for many years." With a sly look, John said, "Since we were friends, I guess he felt it was unnecessary to draw his weapon." Pausing a moment to laugh, John continued, "Through the bank, I had loaned him money many times over the years."

"My friend started stammering, but I finally understood he had been instructed to take me into custody." After much apologetic fumbling, the deputy showed John the papers. "The papers said that I was being charged with 'Grand theft in that he did take, steal, and carry away seventeen hymnals valued at $343.'"

John had to pause in his storytelling as we both bent over in laughter. "What happened then?" I asked after regaining my composure. I had heard the story a hundred times at least, but when one of the participants in those battles told it, it always sounded new.

"Well," John said, "I invited him in to sit on the couch and have a glass of sweet iced tea while I called George Kissinger. He and George talked for a few minutes before my deputy friend hung up and placed the now empty sweet iced tea glass on the table. Still looking sheepish, he stood up to shake my hand and apologize again. I told him to forget it because I knew the source of that warrant."

John chuckled as he concluded, "I guess that's the closest I ever came to being handcuffed and put in jail. Church could be dangerous in those days."

Oh, yes. Just like the Old West.

That story—like so many similar ones—should not be forgotten. They tell of the courage and heroism of men like Edgar Burkholder, John Bazacos, Norman Cullum, and so many other strong men and women who played significant, faithful roles in the earliest beginnings of our church.

In my readings of the Old West, I have discovered that the lives of the principals involved in the original battle at the O.K. Corral on October 26, 1881, in Tombstone, Arizona, had mostly tragic endings.

In that notorious battle, the Earp brothers—Virgil, Wyatt, and Morgan—along with Doc Holliday, defeated a group of suspected cattle rustlers called the "Cowboys." In a very short battle, the Earp brothers dispensed with the Cowboys, but the conflict didn't end there.

Virgil was ambushed in December of that same year. A shotgun blast permanently crippled his left arm. A few months later, Morgan was assassinated.

Wyatt escaped that bullet, even though he was standing nearby, and took over the lawman duties of Virgil as a deputy U.S. marshal and Tombstone town marshal. Wyatt's life has been glorified in popular writings, but the reality of his life was filled with much hardship.

Fortunately, those heroes involved in the "O.K. Corral battles on Strawberry Plains Road" fared much better.

Edgar Burkholder went on to establish a number of churches until he was finally forced to retire in his late nineties for health reasons.

Norman Cullum served Walnut Hills with strong leadership for many years while surviving numerous heart attacks beginning when he was just thirty-nine years of age. Norman even came back to ride his bicycle to work after an episode in which the doctors had declared him brain dead. (But that's another story Norman enjoyed telling; he even left me a copy in his own handwriting.)

John, of course, as I said, continues to tell his stories and wheel out onto his patio at the retirement home to enjoy the lush green grass and sit among the multicolored flowers.

I have always placed a lot of value on good, strong beginnings. However, I have come to realize that it's the finish—the ending—that ultimately matters. Walnut Hills endured a difficult beginning. But the subsequent years have produced much fruit for God's kingdom. In addition, the factions who were part of that early split later renewed their friendship and concern for each other. Only by grace.

I have mentioned just a few of the heroes who have remained faithful in the face of heavy odds during the early years of our church. Thankfully, at each period in the history of Walnut Hills, new heroes with a sense of call have emerged.

And, of course, the ending has not yet been written. We are still on the way, looking eagerly toward what is to come—cheered on by that "great cloud of witnesses": "Therefore, since we are surrounded by such a great cloud of witnesses, let us throw off everything that hinders and the sin that so easily entangles. And let us run with perseverance the race marked out for us..." (Heb 12:1).

I often look around at those gathered for worship on a Sunday morning and wonder, "Who among these is going to be the next hero? Who are the ones willing to run the next lap of the journey?"

The thought of all the possibilities is breathtaking.

# A Lighted Place on Christmas Eve

The first candlelight Communion service at Walnut Hills Baptist Church almost didn't happen. The year was 1971, and we were planning the initial Christmas Eve service in our multipurpose building, which now is the hospitality center. In those early years, the little L-shaped building served as our worship/Sunday school/office space.

My anticipation was high for the beginning of what we hoped would be a continuing tradition for Walnut Hills. But then it came—the worst ice storm in years. The sleet quickly turned into paralyzing ice on December 23.

Should we cancel? It was an agonizing decision, because for months we had all been eagerly awaiting this event.

In spite of the dangerous weather, I wanted desperately to show up and have the lights on and the candles lit just in case anyone came. Our family lived in the parsonage just around the corner on the back end of the church's property, so ours was the shortest trip of all our members.

Still, we crept along on slippery streets until we finally slid through the double front doors on an icy walkway. As soon as we turned on the lights and adjusted the thermostat, the sound of heavy sleet pelting the windowpanes drowned out all other noises.

"Well," I said to our little tribe, which at that time consisted of Jean and me, our daughter Cheryl, and son, Chris, "we'll wait a few minutes, and if no one shows, we'll have a family devotion and go home." I tried to keep the deep disappointment out of my voice. After all, it was Christmas—the time for joy.

Just then, I was startled to hear the stomping of feet and a loud rattling at the front door. A young couple with one small child walked in, smiling as they removed their sleet-covered raincoats.

I greeted them warmly as I walked over to help them. "We weren't sure anyone would show up."

"It wasn't easy," the man replied, chuckling. "But we felt we had to try." He paused and then added, "I saw two more cars pull in behind us."

In the next few minutes, those two cars turned into a caravan, carefully wending its way down Jamestown Road into the ice-covered parking lot in front of our little church building, crouching snugly under the enormous beech tree that was doing its best to protect us from the wintry blast. (Unfortunately, that faithful beech tree eventually died and had to be removed.)

Following a brief Communion service, we lit each other's individual candles, symbolizing the light of Christ scattering throughout a dark—and quite obviously—cold world. The cinderblock walls, which often seemed too harsh for a sanctuary, took on an unusual warmth as the flickering candlelight permeated each corner of our tiny building.

Little did I know that this was the beginning of the spirit that would spread throughout our church family for generations to come—the determination to overcome all obstacles in order to be in their place on Christmas Eve.

In 1973 I came across a resource book titled "New Ways to Worship," compiled by James L. Christensen and just recently published by Fleming H. Revell. In the section of "Celebrative Encounters," I discovered a story by an unknown author about a sixteenth-century duke who built a church called "The Church of the Lamps." I have come across this same story in numerous books over the years since.

According to the legend, the duke had several beautiful daughters whom he loved very much and hated to see leave. When each daughter left, he dreaded the lonely spot that would appear in the home.

During his later years, the old duke decided to preserve his memories by building a beautiful church with one unique feature: There would be no hanging lamps. Instead, worshipers would bring their own bronze lamps to light the little church.

Each person was well aware that if he or she was absent, their place would be dark—as dark as the void in the old duke's home when one of his daughters left.

My adaptation of this story struck a chord with our growing church family. Beginning in 1973, I would tell the story at the conclusion of each Christmas Eve service.

Over the years, this became such a strong tradition that young people who grew up in our church would return home each Christmas Eve so that their place "would not be dark." Prior to my retirement in 2004, attendance on Christmas Eve rivaled our Easter services as chairs would often have to be placed in the aisles for the overflow.

On those rare occasions when some of our people who had moved away were unable to return to Williamsburg for Christmas, I would get a note from them about being heartbroken that their place would be dark on Christmas Eve. But then they would add that they were going to light a candle in a corner of their present home so that, at least somewhere, their light would be shining.

Judy Allan was a high school student when I came as pastor of Walnut Hills in 1969. Her insistence ("No, he is not too young, and if you old folks think so, I'm going to leave the church") was very influential in the church calling me at twenty-eight years of age with no pastoral experience.

But in 1979, Judy, who had never been out of Virginia, moved to Muncie, Indiana, with her husband, Ross, and their three-year-old son, Scot. Deeply homesick, Judy called her mother—affectionally known by the children in our Learning Center as "Miss Lene."

Telling her mother how she dreaded her "corner" being dark that Christmas Eve and how she could not bear the thought of not hearing the story, Miss Lene told her to call the Haywoods: "You know how much they love you."

Jean called me to the phone when she learned that it was Judy and that she wanted to hear the story—even though she already knew it by heart. When I concluded reading the story to her over the phone, Judy asked, "Do you think someone could light a candle for me this Christmas Eve?"

So at the beginning of the service, I asked someone to light a candle just for Judy. She said later what wonderful peace and joy she felt when she learned of that. (A devotional written in 2013 by Linda Ward, our minister of education, refreshed my memory of these events. Linda always did an excellent job of preparing our Advent devotional booklet each Christmas.)

Some traditions block progress. Some traditions hinder us from moving on toward personal growth and a better place. Then there are other traditions that promote growth and deepen our experience of the spiritual. Such were the traditions surrounding our Christmas Eve services.

They say that Christmas comes to Williamsburg when all the lights go on in the buildings along Duke of Gloucester Street and a huge display of fireworks lights up the night sky in what is known as the "Grand Illumination." For me, Christmas always came to Williamsburg when I told the story of "The Church of the Lamps" and all our individual candles were lit and we scattered to bring light to all the dark places along our journey toward Mullinix.

Now, all these years later, folks still stop me in the church hallways to ask for a copy of our version of "The Church of the Lamps" to send to their daughters and sons who are in new places and need the comfort of a little bit of home at Christmas.

There was a time in the history of the people of Israel when they questioned if they could sing a song in a new land. A captive, exiled people seriously doubted if they could bring the joy of home along with them: "By the rivers of Babylon we sat and wept when we remembered Zion. There on the poplars we hung our harps, for there our captors asked us for songs, our tormentors demanded songs of joy; they said, 'Sing us one of the songs of Zion!' How can we sing the songs of the Lord while in a foreign land?" (Ps 137:1–4).

But they, along with all those young people in our church who grew up with the story, discovered that home was not so much a place as a Presence—a breathtaking Presence who places a song on our tongues and a light in our hearts no matter where we are along the journey to Mullinix.

# Success at Last

"Well, Pastor," the friendly voice said enthusiastically, "you did it. You're a success."

It isn't often you can give the exact date and time you became a success. Was this one of those times? It was November 6, 1987, at 11:36 in the morning—a beautiful sunny day. Couldn't have picked better weather to become a success.

A huge crane was carefully placing the steeple onto its base, waiting expectantly on top of the almost completed sanctuary of Walnut Hills Baptist Church.

A large number of people were standing anywhere they could find an empty space, watching this tedious operation. Some were gathered at the edge of the woods across Jamestown Road. Others were spilling into the road while still more were squeezing into the front parking lot, pressing as close to the action as the insurance folks would allow.

I was probably standing too close, claiming "pastoral privilege," which is being recognized in fewer and fewer places these days. That doesn't bother me, of course, since I never asked for nor expected any special privilege for holding a particular position. I've always felt the character of a person should be valued much more than any position he or she might hold—and that includes the highest office in our country.

A tug at my elbow suddenly pulled my attention away from the steeple swinging like a pendulum from the steel cables of the crane. As I turned, I looked into the smiling eyes of a familiar face, a local reporter from the *Virginia Gazette*. He was holding a pad and pen while trying to keep the strap of his expensive camera from sliding off his left shoulder.

"Well, Pastor," he said, "you did it."

"How's that?" I asked.

"You're finally a success," he continued, his smile growing wider. "Very few in this community thought you folks would ever establish a permanent colony here on Jamestown Road. But you succeeded."

I don't know exactly why I glanced down at my watch then—but that's why I know the time—11:36. I think I looked at my watch to give myself an opportunity to formulate a response. His words had grated on my good spirits. It was a joyful moment. But somehow he was using the wrong words—especially for someone who made his living by choosing the right words.

Oh, I could understand why he said what he did. Eight months prior to my arrival as pastor in 1969, the little church had endured an acrimonious split after years of serious quarreling. The community had given up on them. The first visitor I entertained after I had moved my family to Williamsburg was a local pastor who came to warn me rather than welcome me.

We had barely taken our seats in the living room of the parsonage when my colleague blurted out, "I just came by to tell you that you're wasting your time."

"Maybe so," I replied, after pausing to regain my composure. "But I am certain this is where God wants me. So I think I'm going to stick around a while to see what he's going to do with it."

I had no idea at the time that the "sticking around a while" would last thirty-five years—nor that we would be erecting a stately steeple seventeen years later.

So I could understand the reporter's words. He had meant them as a compliment, celebrating the fact that we had overcome many obstacles to reach this moment.

But I couldn't shake my irritation that he felt this steeple was a sign we had become a success. I felt we had succeeded in being Christ's heart and hands in many ways and many places throughout the previous seventeen years.

For instance, when our members took turns sitting by the bed of a stranger, holding her hand as she died. She had been vacationing in Williamsburg away from family when a heart attack struck her down. The hospital called, and we became Christ's family for her.

Or when a couple in our church discovered a poverty-stricken family during our annual Christmas meal deliveries and continued to bring food for the mother and three children throughout the entire next year.

When a young boy and his sister, abused by divorcing parents, found a safe home with a church family.

When small children learned about Jesus and older adults discovered the tenets of the faith through people who dedicated their lives to studying and teaching.

When a group of women and men led a Bible study in a local jail, sometimes welcomed and sometimes shunned or ignored.

When homesick college students were "adopted" by church families and given a place to belong.

When anyone anywhere offered a word of hope to the lonely, the loveless, the weak, the wounded, the lost, the powerful, the self-righteous, the church was succeeding in carrying on the work of the risen Lord.

Those were not steeple-raising moments with hundreds of onlookers crowded together on Jamestown Road. These events took place in quiet, out-of-the-way places by anonymous disciples who only wanted to respond to human need in Christ's name.

So in my mind, success for a church family is receiving grace and love and healing from Christ in such abundant portions that it spills over into the surrounding community and the larger world. Any success the Walnut Hills family achieved began long before that steeple was placed on top of our new building.

I understood why it was difficult for the reporter to understand that. We live in a steeple-raising society. The big, the loud, the showy, the extravagant—these are the signs of success. It takes a great deal of wakefulness and sensitivity to resist the temptation of measuring success by society's standards.

Maybe that was something of what Jesus was talking about in Matthew when he warned us not to give alms like the hypocrites who blow a trumpet in order to call attention to their good deeds: "'But when you give to the needy, do not let your left hand know what your right hand is doing, so that your giving may be in secret. Then your Father, who sees what is done in secret, will reward you" (Matt 6:3–4).

If the secret places are where alms are to be given and where the Father gives his rewards, maybe we should be wary of making too much of steeple-raising moments. If the Father sees in secret and judges in secret, we must be cautious of public trumpet-blowing.

The reporter took a nice front-page picture of the steeple settling into its resting place. He also wrote a nice story about our church. I was grateful for that. I was most grateful, however, that he did not use the word *success* in his story.

I must confess that it was breathtaking to watch that majestic steeple take its place on top of our new sanctuary. But in no way could it be called a true measure of our success as a Christian church.

# I'm Going to Take Your Pants

"What are you going to do?" Ken Reining was staring at my water-soaked suit pants dripping on the office floor, which doubled as a dressing room for our first baptistery. Ken always found the humor in any situation and had a funny story for every event. On this morning, however, standing before his waterlogged pastor, Ken was speechless.

In an earlier story, I told about the unfortunate events that occurred when our submersible baptistery heater disengaged at low water levels. At such times, the water temperature never reached a comfortable range—"comfortable" meaning any temperature above freezing.

But problems also occurred when the water level rose too high. I've noticed that life doesn't go well when lived in the extremities. That is certainly true of extreme low and high baptistery water levels.

All those scheduled to be baptized on this particular Sunday were adults, so the baptismal committee thought it would be a good idea if the water level rose to the middle of my chest. Their thinking was that I wouldn't have to bend over quite so far while immersing the grownups—most of whom were taller than I am. Theoretically, it would be easier for everyone.

Theoretically, they were right. Practically, they were wrong. Sad how so many of our wonderful theories fall flat when put into practice.

The waders I used during those days came up to my armpits. But they were secondhand, and the straps had a tendency to sag even after I adjusted them. That was before one of the metal buttons fell off completely. So as I walked into the water, I noticed that the water line crept perilously close to the top of those sagging, well-used rubber waders.

The first person I baptized was a slender young woman. I gently lowered her backward into the water with a sigh of relief as my waders did their job of keeping me dry. Two more of our skinniest candidates were baptized without incident.

But then came Ken Reining. Ken was not as large as both of us became later; nevertheless, his waist was still a few inches thicker than the svelte converts who were baptized before him. As Ken stepped into the water, I breathed a sigh of relief when the water level rested two inches beneath the top of my waders.

That relief was short-lived.

When I stood from lowering Ken into the water, the top of my waders scooped up a generous portion of the sacred water. I struggled to maintain my poise as I felt the lukewarm water soak my pants and boxer shorts and finally caress the cotton dress socks I still wore as a novice baptizer.

Ordinarily, all of that would not have been a big deal. I would simply have gone home and changed clothes. It wasn't the first time I had been soaking wet while fully dressed. Except in this instance, I was scheduled to return to the front of the sanctuary and conclude the service with a hymn of commitment followed by a benediction.

My drenched socks squished in each water-logged foot of the waders as I climbed down the rickety wooden baptistery steps. Ken had seen the water spill over the top of my waders just as he emerged from the water, so he was waiting for me, already fully dressed in dry clothes.

After sliding the wader straps off my shoulders, I reached over and slipped into my dry suit jacket, which I had carefully placed on a hanger before entering the baptistery. Unfortunately, the jacket did little to cover my clinging pants, although it did a passable job of hiding the bottom half of my dripping tie and white shirt.

"I'm absolutely soaked," I said, stating the obvious, as preachers are sometimes prone to do. "And I've got to go out there, give the invitation, and pronounce the benediction."

After staring at me for a few moments in speechless sympathy, Ken finally found his voice just as his irrepressible sense of humor was also returning. Choking on his laughter, Ken asked, "What are you going to do?"

That was when I again stated the obvious. This time, however, I did so with a great deal of purposeful intensity, leaving no room for argument. "Ken, I'm going to take your pants!"

He had given up trying to suppress his laughter but was able to mumble, "Guess there's nothing else to do." Without hesitating, Ken began slipping out of his pants.

So Ken Reining spent the remainder of that morning worship service huddling in his boxers behind a partition in a corner of the dressing room—hoping no one walked in before his pastor returned with his pants.

When I told that story the following week to our people, everyone confessed that they had not even noticed my mismatched jacket and ill-fitting pants. I took that as a sign that we had come a long way in becoming a real church family.

At my "trial sermon" a few years earlier, a young woman said she liked my new suit. "How did you know it was new?" I asked, frantically searching for an overlooked price tag.

"Well," she said, "I noticed that the cuffs on your pants legs didn't have the sharp creases you get from most dry cleaners." Smiling with satisfaction, she continued, "So I assumed your suit had never been to the cleaners and your wife had hemmed and ironed the new pants in preparation for today."

With panicked eyes, I searched for the nearest exit. If these people were going to look at me that closely, I wouldn't last a month with all my rookie roughness and casual creases.

So on the Sunday following the baptismal soaking, it was deeply reassuring that no one had even noticed when I stood before them in sockless shoes and mismatched clothing. It was comforting to know that our relationship had become much more important than outward appearances.

I guess I should have expected it, fond as I am of this verse in 1 Peter: "Above all, love each other deeply, because love covers over a multitude of sins" (4:8).

After all these years, I am still amazed at how many little and big things love can gently cover with a thick shell of compassion.

This experience also reminded me that, on the way to Mullinix, I may have to walk a few steps in someone else's pants in order to be reminded of such breathtaking love.

# Not an Easy Love

It was on an Advent morning in 1986 when Robert Hall and I stood in the unfinished sanctuary and watched through a side window as a large funnel sent wet cement mix racing to its destination.

"They sure do make it easy these days," Robert said, shaking his head. Robert had been our church custodian for over thirty years, but mostly he was a friend and a valued part of our church family.

When I retired as pastor of Walnut Hills after thirty-five years, Robert came up to me at our retirement celebration and said with a warm smile, "Jerry, if I had known you were going to last for thirty-five years, I would have stayed on another two years. Don't like it that you outlasted me," Robert concluded with a laugh.

Robert preceded me in his arrival at Walnut Hills—serving as custodian in the little mission prior to our building a larger structure on Jamestown Road. We both had seen the church through many changes and transitions and growth stages.

In fall 1984, our attendance in Sunday school and worship services experienced significant increases. The average Sunday school attendance was over 200, and our worship services ranged between 300 and 400. On special services like Easter, we rose to 500-plus, far above the fire marshal's approved capacity. (I do hope the statute of limitations has passed on that particular crime.)

Those are not very large statistics, except for the fact that all of our activities were taking place in our first little L-shaped building constructed in October 1969 and intended to hold much smaller numbers.

So in April 1985, we decided to move ahead with the construction of a new building. Many folks were persuaded it was time to bite that large bullet when a visitor passed out during our Easter service.

The ceiling was so low in that first building that when it was full of people, the available oxygen grew thin. If anyone's lungs were already compromised, breathing became difficult.

One of our irrepressible members, Tom Sublett, was ushering on that fateful Easter morning and began rushing toward the back row to assist the collapsed visitor. Fortunately, just before he arrived, the man regained consciousness.

One of the other ushers, Tom Campbell, told me later that Sublett, who could never resist an opportunity at humor, whispered to him, "He has risen!"

We had no shortage of humorists in those days. But we also had people with vision and dreams. For some time we had been discussing the options of enlarging our present building or constructing a new sanctuary.

One of our women leaders said on the way out that Easter morning, "If the Lord ever gave us a sign." That sentiment was echoed by many others—especially those who had been sitting near our fainting visitor.

At our next business meeting, the vote was unanimous to begin drawing up plans for a new sanctuary.

On this Advent morning, as Robert and I watched the sloppy concrete rush through its flexible funnel, he said thoughtfully, "Back when I drove a cement truck, we had to use a crane and lift buckets in order to reach those high, hard-to-get-at places." Then he added, "This is much, much easier."

Earlier, my thoughts had been on God's Christmas gift of love as I was preparing a series of Advent sermons. I responded, "But isn't it amazing that God could not find an easier way?" Robert looked at me silently, as he often did while waiting for the preacher to finish his sermon. Robert was a deacon in his church and a man of deep faith.

"To rescue us, God could find no other way than to give his only Son, entering the world of humanity and then suffering death on a cross."

"That's the truth," Robert said emphatically, as we resumed silently watching the liquid concrete flowing easily toward its destination.

That conversation with Robert came rushing back a few years later when I was watching the Christmas story told from the perspective of the kindergarten class in our Learning Center.

This year, I was paying close attention to the shepherds, since the shepherds who received the announcement of Jesus's birth were the focus for my Sunday sermon. Those kindergarteners made cute little shepherds—scrubbed as pink and clean as their mothers could make them. Their bathrobes were colorful and spotlessly clean.

As I walked into the sanctuary, two of the little shepherds handed me a program. Just that small movement stirred the pleasant aroma of Downy fabric softener.

When the pageant ended, I said to one of the teachers, "That was great. I always enjoy this Christmas pageant."

She said, smiling, "It's a lot of work, but it's the highlight of the Christmas season for me too."

"There's only one small problem," I continued, as she paused to listen. "The shepherds smelled much too good."

I thought I was being funny, but alarm spread over the young teacher's face as she leaned toward me. "Shhhh," she said, quickly placing her forefinger to her pursed lips. "Please don't let the children hear you say that. You can't imagine how much they love bad odors. Anything that stinks cracks up the entire class. It's hard to restore order."

Laughing, I promised to honor her request. But on Sunday I did feel it was necessary to tell the worshipers how badly the New Testament shepherds smelled. They really had no choice, being dirty outcasts unwelcome in respectable society.

The nearest shower was over 2,000 years away, and their hot days and long nights spent tending smelly sheep were enough to defeat the best efforts of the most potent cologne.

I do love the "Hallmark version" of Christmas—the scrubbed, squeaky-clean version of Christmas. But there was nothing clean or easy about that first Christmas.

The stable where Jesus was born no doubt smelled of animal waste. And we have no way of knowing how recently a slobbering animal had eaten out of the manger in which Mary laid the Son of God.

All of this, of course, foreshadowed the cross. There was no instrument of death harder or dirtier than the cross. Jesus was excruciatingly aware of that. His prayer on the Mount of Olives left no doubt of his full understanding of where his earthly life was to end: "'Father, if you are willing, take this cup from me; yet not my will, but yours be done'.... And being in anguish, he prayed more earnestly, and his sweat was like drops of blood falling to the ground." (Luke 22:42, 44).

God loving us so much that he gave his "only Son that we might not perish but have eternal life" was not an easy love. It began in a smelly stable and ended on an atrociously brutal and dirty cross. There seemed to be no easier way.

Earlier in the same week of my conversation with Robert, one of the young women in our church, expecting her first baby, was not having an easy time of it either. In fact, she had experienced agonizingly long weeks of obstacles and complications and pain and even the possibility of losing the baby—or her own life.

But then, late on Wednesday afternoon, I walked into the hospital room to find the young mother looking down lovingly at the baby cradled in her arms.

"Now we can enjoy Christmas," she said, smiling as she reached up to grasp the hand of her adoring husband. "The baby is here. Everything will be all right."

It was not an easy love. At times it was breathtakingly painful. But rejoice! The baby is here! Everything will be all right.

# Part Two

A Breathtaking Journey

Is Sometimes Just Fun

# Lessons from the Mule

The prospective bride looked highly anxious as her eyes shifted between me and her fiancé, who was watching us both with a strained smile.

"We didn't do so good, did we?" Her lovely face was hopeful but wary.

We were in the middle of a series of premarital counseling sessions, reviewing the personality inventory they had both filled out earlier. I had explained this was not a test to fail or pass. However, their answers to a large number of the questions were so different that they both felt they had failed.

Were their differences so extreme that I was going to refuse to marry them?

Chuckling, I said, "No, that's your decision. I have discovered that many differences can be successfully negotiated as long as your basic worldviews are the same. As long as the way you see the world—especially what you value—is similar, then other differences are manageable—even helpful. The last research I saw said that approximately seventy-five percent of couples marry opposites."

I then told them about the couple I had married who were so identical in every area that I could not imagine conflict ever occurring. So I was surprised when around their first anniversary, they called and said they were having problems and needed to see me. Their problem: "We are so much alike that we are boring each other to death."

The couple relaxed a little, and I continued, "Besides, look at the mule."

"The what?" they exclaimed simultaneously.

They were both city folk, recent graduates from the College of William & Mary. Smart people but totally ignorant about important subjects like mules.

I had to give them a quick lesson. As I have indicated before, I have a fondness for mules—having plowed and spent many summer days with them in my younger years. But this lesson had nothing to do with my pleasant memory of mules. Rather, understanding the mule was critical to the future of this couple's life together.

Perhaps not too surprisingly, it was news to them that the mule is a cross between a female horse and a male donkey. I felt it was important that I share my thoughts about that first diminutive donkey courted by the beautiful stately horse.

The scene is easy to imagine. "What? Me?" exclaimed the donkey. "You want me to be the father of your children! Me, just a common jackass?"

The donkey quickly lowered his head and pawed the ground shyly with his left front hoof. He was terribly embarrassed that he had failed to call himself by the name given him by the great namer of all things—and "Jack" had slipped carelessly into the nickname his friends had given him.

The horse was kind enough to pretend she had not heard, extending a tentative hoof of her own toward her chosen as she, too, pawed gently at the ground and replied, "Yes. I know we haven't known each other long—just kind of glancing at each other as we passed in the pasture. But I have sensed a certain chemistry and would like to marry you and have your child."

"I can't believe this," the donkey muttered to himself. But this was too good to let slip away. He was accustomed to chasing the female donkeys around the pasture—sometimes for days—until they agreed to marry him. He was also aware that he was not the most handsome of suitors. But now this beautiful creature was coming to him with an incredible proposition. He had observed that donkeys were not nearly as fast as horses, but this horse was so fast that it took his breath away.

With a mighty effort, the donkey slowed his breathing, so as not to hyperventilate, and replied—much louder than he had intended—"Hee-haw! Hee-haw! I mean, wow! Yes! Yes! By all that is within me—yes!"

Suddenly fearing he was being a little too eager and failing to adhere to the male mantra of feigning indifference when the female is dancing around in excitement, the donkey lowered his head slowly to crop the nearest tuft of grass.

The horse sighed in relief as she replied, "Well, I'm glad that's settled." Then she, too, began nibbling at a patch of lush grass. They were quiet for a while except for the sound of ripping grass as each wondered about the next move.

Just then, a thought struck the donkey. "But what shall we call our child?"

As with most prospective mothers, the horse replied, "I've given this a lot of thought. We shall call him 'The Mule,' for he will be neither horse nor donkey but will possess the best qualities of us both."

The donkey was greatly intrigued as he stared blearily down the hill toward the barn. "'The Mule,' he muttered to himself. 'I like that.'"

Then his imagination began to soar. What a marvelous creature their offspring would be—possessing his strength, intelligence, endurance, and surefootedness—to name just a few of his better qualities. Combining that with the athleticism, lovely curves, flowing mane, and incredible beauty of this creature standing before him—well, it was almost too much to contemplate.

Shaking his head vigorously to make sure he wasn't dreaming, the donkey could only stare into the distance with wondering, unseeing eyes.

"And the rest is history," I said, looking up at the puzzled expressions of the couple sitting before me. "The horse and the donkey lived happily ever after. And sure enough, their union produced 'The Mule'—a wondrous creature possessing the best qualities of them both."

The young couple seemed to be so enthralled by my story that they were momentarily rendered speechless. I continued, "You know, I've often thought the mule would be an ideal mascot for the church—as well as a goal toward which all good marriages should strive."

Seeing they were still speechless, staring at me dumbly, I added, "Remember how Paul characterized the church in his great chapter on gifts?" (1 Cor 12).

It was obvious they had omitted the New Testament class at W&M, along with the one on "The Mule," so I proceeded to enlighten them.

"Paul talks about how all the parts of the human body are different, but when they come together—each bringing its own uniqueness—they form a healthy functioning body."

Both of them were nodding slightly, so I assumed they were eager for me to continue: "That's the way he also says it is with a healthy church. The differing gifts of each member are united so the church can function efficiently."

They had been silent for a long time. I asked, "Do you see how that relates to your marriage?"

"I think so," the bride-to-be began hesitantly, with the smallest hint of a dawning light in her eyes. "We are very different—as that personality inventory showed." She glanced briefly at her fiancé and smiled nervously before continuing, "But when we combine our differences—our different gifts and personalities—it can work and maybe even create something good and perhaps an offspring even better than we are as individuals?" She said this more like a question than a statement.

Her fiancé looked at her with wonder. "Yeah," he said slowly, confirming my suspicions that he was going to be the donkey in this relationship, daily surprised by his wife's ideas, trying hard to keep up. "I guess that's about right."

"That's *exactly* right!" I cried enthusiastically. Standing, I said, "You look a little tired. Think about our conversation today, and we'll get together again at the same time next week."

Just before exiting my study, the young woman turned with a wry smile and said, "Pastor, I didn't see a picture of 'The Mule' on the wall in the hallway. What happened to your mascot?"

"Well," I said, returning her smile, "I mentioned it to the deacons, and they told me to take a couple weeks off and go rest down by the river."

I heard them both laughing as their steps echoed down the empty hallway before ending with the clang of the front door opening and closing.

Leaning back in my chair, I muttered to myself, "The road to Mullinix has challenging moments and moments that take your breath away. Then there are times when it's just fun."

# The Proper Clergy Dress Code

"**P**astor, loosen up. Take off your jacket. It's hot in here."

Those words came from a concerned deacon who was encouraging me to follow the summer dress code of no jackets and ties—just short-sleeved shirts. As usual, I replied, "I appreciate your concern, but I'm okay."

Baptists have always liked to simplify things—especially their dress code. No robes for clergy except for weddings, and even then the bride is given the choice. Usually, the choir sheds its robes in the summer when the air-conditioning has trouble competing with the sweltering humidity.

We are always shooting for comfort anywhere we can find it in such an uncomfortable faith as Christianity.

In some of the more informal contemporary churches, worship leaders have adopted jeans and untucked shirts as a sign of identification with the "come-as-you-are" worshipers and those disenchanted by traditional pastors.

In spite of all this, I always wear a jacket. But that has more to do with a traumatic experience I suffered as a young boy growing up in Calvary Baptist Church in rural North Carolina than it does with being a stiff-necked traditionalist.

At the time, we had a very likable, enthusiastic giant of a pastor who commanded attention by the volume of his voice, the wideness of his smile, and the frenetic waving of his arms. That method of keeping us awake served him well—until one Sunday evening in August during our second worship service of the day.

Our dedicated, lifetime deacons were certain that two services on Sunday were required somewhere within the laws of almighty God—even if they couldn't quite put their finger on the exact text.

On this particular night, the thermometer registered in the nineties—even after sunset—with hundreds of insects but no breeze coming through the open windows of our little sanctuary. Quite naturally, our beloved pastor decided it was time to remove his jacket.

We were accustomed to such a ritual, but on this occasion it was obvious from the way his white shirt quickly plastered to his sweat-drenched torso that he was not wearing a t-shirt. That was okay too, because very few of us men and boys wore t-shirts in the summer, and most of us went totally shirtless.

But suddenly I was desperately wishing our pastor had chosen to wear a t-shirt. As he made a dramatic swoop with his right arm, turning his body one-quarter of a circle, emphasizing the gravity of his point, I was startled to catch a fleeting glimpse of back hair.

"Oh, no," I whispered, quickly bowing my head behind the pew in front of our Sunday night family pew. I say "Sunday night family pew" because my parents sang in the choir on Sunday morning. Occasionally, there was no choir in the evening service, so we sat together on our favorite pew—five rows back on the right side of the aisle.

Like my mother, I have always had a fairly reliable sense of foreboding. Suddenly, that sixth sense had kicked into overdrive.

Uttering a silent prayer that my eyes had deceived me, I was sadly face-to-face with the harsh reality that this was one of those prayers God was choosing not to answer in the affirmative. Suddenly, our pastor's massive body twisted a full 180 degrees with a spirited swing of his right arm, revealing a horrible sight.

An audible gasp swept through the congregation as we saw that his well-worn white shirt had endured one washing too many and had finally surrendered to our pastor's enthusiastic proclamation of the Word. A four-inch-wide split extended all the way down the shirt's back until finally, blessedly, ending in the tuck at his waist.

An expansive back as hairy as any I have ever seen on a member of the human species lay fully exposed before the horrified eyes of a church full of "cream of the crop" Sunday evening worshipers.

Some of the ladies quickly bowed their heads, demurely covering their faces with the handheld fans promising a "reliable, dignified funeral service" if such responsibilities were placed within the "capable, experienced hands" of the trustworthy institution that had provided the fans.

For a moment I thought I might be needing the services of that trustworthy institution much earlier than I had anticipated.

Not surprisingly, my mother started laughing. Mother always had a wonderful way of finding humor in our human foibles without actually laughing at the unfortunate victim. For instance, she always roared with laughter when anyone fell—most especially herself. (She would have loved *America's Funniest Home Videos*.) I can still hear my father's admonishment: "Ina, that isn't funny. You could have hurt yourself badly"— which caused mother to laugh even harder as she struggled to get up.

Now she was trying hard to hide her laughter as she placed her hand over her face and shuffled in her seat. But she could not keep the occasional tear from sliding down her cheeks with the strain of it all.

My father was watching Mother out of the corner of his right eye with that way he had of peeking at something off to the side without actually turning his head—so as to maintain as much dignity as possible. I suppose it was also intended as a silent request that Mother stifle her amusement.

I was glad Mother could laugh, but I was too mortified to join her on this occasion, suffering from the severe embarrassment of the young who attach far too much importance to outward appearances. I've noticed, sadly, some folks never grow out of that proclivity.

No one heard anything our pastor said after that, of course, but our eyes never left him as some perverse attraction drew us toward catching another glimpse of that broad, muscular back covered with thick, curly black hair.

Relief swept over me at the end of most sermons—especially during my young years at a period in church circles when the value of preaching was partially measured by its length. If the sermon was too short, it was assumed that the pastor had received very little inspiration from the Holy Spirit that week.

Likewise, we felt we were cheating the Lord out of a chance to move hearts unless we sang all four and sometimes five verses of the invitational hymn. Usually I didn't mind, but this time I couldn't wait for the hymn to end and our pastor could slip on his jacket and hide that deeply disturbing sight.

I hope you're beginning to understand why I always wear a jacket when standing before a group of people, no matter how unbearably hot it might be. My back isn't nearly as hairy as my boyhood pastor's—which I'm sure has more to do with a genetic phenomenon than a variance in evolutionary levels—but I still prefer keeping my mostly hairless back skin under cover.

Maybe you think that's an overreaction after all these years, but you weren't a shy, overly sensitive nine-year-old boy at Calvary Baptist Church on that hot August night in 1949 when a revered pastor's hairy back was laid bare for all the world to see.

It's an image I can never erase. The scars remain.

As I've grown older, I've noticed that most scars have a remarkable ability to endure. I still have a scar just above my kneecap where a sizable plug of my tender five-year-old flesh was removed by the end point of a crosscut saw, which I tried to hold steady as my father labored on the other end to cut up a tree for our firewood.

My brother has a scar the length of a finger on his right hand where I split it open with a dropped rock while we were loading our little metal red wagon.

Physical scars are difficult to hide. Most efforts to hide emotional scars seem equally unsuccessful.

She came to see me on several occasions over many years. Both parents had been alcoholics when she was growing up. Now in her late middle age, she was very successful in her career and much beloved by her husband and family and co-workers.

But the scars remained. "Pastor Jerry, I have forgiven them, and I know God has forgiven them. But I will always be scarred by those years of daily insecurity, abject poverty, and the continuous emotional and physical abuse."

Each time we talked, she could never hold back the tears. Traumatic scars always seem to live on far beyond the place where the cause of those scars has been forgiven.

In his beautiful psalm of thanksgiving for God's goodness, the psalmist assures us that "as far as the east is from the west, so far has he removed our transgressions from us." (103:12).

My breath catches a little every time I read those words. God's forgiveness completely removes our transgressions—not only from our sight but from anywhere near us geographically. Our sins have been hidden from us.

But I still can't escape the sadness of seeing a flood of tears over emotional scars, which are much more difficult to hide.

Makes me think that along the Mullinix journey—while I remain deeply thankful for the forgiveness of God and others—I must be careful to leave as few scars as possible.

Scars that still, on occasion, take our breath away.

# Fi-Fi's Fountain

I thought the receptionist was kidding when she said, "Fi-Fi will clean your teeth today." When I realized she was serious, I wondered if a large French poodle had been specially trained as a dental hygienist. I knew robots were fast taking over our jobs. Maybe our jobs were also going to the dogs.

But Fi-Fi was no dog. In fact, she was an attractive blonde with a large smile encircled with a thick coating of hot pink lipstick. Things were not shaping up as I had envisioned.

Now I have never objected to attractive middle-aged blondes (or blondes of any age, for that matter) with hot pink lipstick—unless I'm sitting in a dentist's chair with my mouth open listening to a disgusting gurgle emanating from the end of a curved tube held in place by a tongue that suddenly feels strangely out of place.

The only comforting part of the whole ordeal was the pleasant hint of honey-suckle-scented perfume that wafted my way when Fi-Fi leaned over with her twirling needle to remove the six-month accumulation of plaque from my teeth.

"Take that cup of water and spit in the fountain," Fi-Fi said in a friendly yet commanding tone, which held a hint of threat if I did not follow orders correctly and quickly.

Leaning over the little white fountain and spitting sideways was difficult—especially since I have not made it a practice of spitting in front of attractive middle-aged blondes with hot pink lipstick. That just isn't my style.

This spitting order was made periodically over the next few minutes until I realized the cup was empty. "No more water," I said shyly, suddenly incapable of making a rational decision or solving the simplest of puzzles on my own. "Oh, no!" I thought. "It's happening again. Why do I always revert to being a helpless child in a dentist's office?"

"Push the button nearest you," Fi-Fi said as she placed the drill on its hanger and turned to walk into the hallway.

I was pleased that as soon as I pressed the button, a clear stream of water started flowing into my empty cup. Panic suddenly replaced pleasure, however, as my cup filled rapidly. I gulped it down hurriedly in order to get the cup back under the flow, which was now a steady, unending stream.

Thankfully, I noticed a little button that read "Stop," and I pressed it firmly. But nothing stopped. The water kept coming and coming, and I kept gulping and gulping in a vain attempt to keep the room from flooding.

With a last desperate move, I pulled up on the button I had pressed down in hopes that maybe taking a backward approach might make the water stop. It did not. Instead, the little button pulled all the way out, and I sat there with the button in one hand, gulping cups full of water with the other.

I had read somewhere that you can drown by drinking too much water. I was definitely not feeling well.

I think I can speak for most men when I say we do not like to appear foolish in the presence of members of the opposite sex—especially attractive middle-aged blondes wearing hot pink lipstick and smelling like honeysuckle on a dewy spring morning.

But I had no choice. I needed help. I saw out of the corner of my left eye—the one nearest the overflowing fountain—that Fi-Fi was talking and giggling on her cellphone, totally unaware that a catastrophe was occurring right under her watch.

"Hey!" I called out in a whispered shout between deep gulps of water. "Need some help in here." But Fi-Fi was giggling too loudly to hear me.

I continued to swallow rapidly in an effort to clear my vocal passages, and I called out again, "Major flood in here!" Again, it came out as a whispered shout. I wasn't eager to have my humiliation broadcast throughout the office.

I don't think she ever heard me, but Fi-Fi finally placed her phone in the pocket of her lime green smock and walked into the water-logged treatment room. "Watch the floor," I said sheepishly. "It's a little slick."

I still don't know how she did it, but Fi-Fi simultaneously lunged to hit the button that now miraculously stopped the flow of water while grabbing a big suction thingamajig to drain the water out of the overflowing white bowl.

Finally, laying the suction aside and beginning to mop up the water, Fi-Fi gave me one of those looks that time-traveled me back to first grade at Mt. Gilead Elementary School. Like I said, I'm not sure what it is, but going to a dentist always makes me feel like a clueless first-grader. Maybe it's because everyone in the room knows more than I do about what's going on and I'm waiting uncomfortably for my next instruction, which I may or may not be able to carry out. Guess I have to leave the full explanation to my psychiatrist.

Just like in first grade, I didn't have to wait long for the next command. In truth, also like in first grade, the instruction sounded a lot like an admonishment. "Looks like you kept pushing the button on the left," Fi-Fi muttered out of the side of her painted mouth while still mopping the floor.

"No, ma'am." I was at least thirty years older than this dental assistant, but "ma'am" seemed like the right thing to say.

"No, ma'am," I continued quietly. "I pushed the one on the right." But she was looking at me with that teacher look, which left no room for debate. "I mean, ah, yes, ma'am. Maybe I did." I did not want to endure the added humiliation of having to stand in the corner for "back-talking."

Perhaps noticing my anxiety, Fi-Fi said in a slightly softer tone, "Now, just relax and put your hands in your lap." Turning toward the counter to her right, she asked— well, it was intended to be a question, but was most definitely a command— "Would you like to hold this nice new toothbrush? And what about this roll of floss?" She didn't say it, but my first-grade ears heard, "Idle hands are the devil's workshop."

Standing over me again, Fi-Fi looked down and tried to smile, but it's awfully hard to smile when your mouth is permanently set in a straight line.

"Do you floss, Jerry?"

"No ma'am. I mean, yes, ma'am. Ah...sometimes—Sundays."

With my head bowed in a submissive position—I've watched dogs do that when they wanted no misunderstanding over who possessed the authority— I suddenly noticed that Fi-Fi was wearing ankle bracelets. I knew then I most certainly had not time-traveled back to first grade. My teacher was an excellent, old-school instructor who gave my educational pursuits a solid foundation, for which I have always been grateful. But the school was short of teachers that year and had begged her to come out of retirement even though she had already worked well past retirement age. She was a stern, well-seasoned teacher, but she most definitely never wore ankle bracelets.

Fi-Fi's ankles were quite slender, and her shoes looked expensive and stylish. My first-grade teacher's shoes were designed to give comfort to bunions and fallen arches and weak ankles. Those bunions and fallen arches and weak ankles were probably why she never walked to the back of the room to deliver punishment to those on the back row, preferring instead to throw chalk and blackboard erasers toward the offenders.

Unfortunately, her actual targets were seldom hit, and many an innocent soul was startled out of a daydream by an errant eraser striking them on the side of the head. That was the beginning of my education concerning the unfairness of life.

Finally, the dentist came in to check Fi-Fi's work. Finding it acceptable, he said he would see me in six months. Since the dentist and I were friends, we usually had a long conversation. But maybe he noticed the wet floor and wanted to get out as quickly as possible before slipping and breaking a hip.

Needless to say, after pausing at the billing office, I exited the building as quickly as possible. I wasn't quick enough, however, to avoid hearing some very unprofessional snickers scattered throughout the office. I could easily imagine the scene: "Just had this preacher in here. Flooded the office. Guess he thought I needed baptizing."

I'm fairly certain that happened, because a sudden explosion of laughter accentuated the front door slapping me on my backside as I hurried out.

"Well, Fi-Fi, you just wait. Next time I'm here, I'm going to tell on you. I'm going to tell how foolish you made me feel. The dentist is a good friend of mine! I'm going to tell!" Obviously, I hadn't quite shaken off my first-grade mentality as I climbed into the car.

Predictably, two miles or so down the road, I started laughing uproariously. My grandson Brent often says, "Papa, you crack yourself up." He's right. There seems to be no limit to how ridiculously funny I can seem to myself.

But then—right in the middle of my hilarity—a remarkable thought struck me: "No matter how ridiculous I act, *God has never made me feel like a first-grader.* In spite of the fact that he knows my every silly, dumb, ugly thought, God has never made me feel *small.*"

I have often felt remorseful and guilty in his presence, which I think is healthy. But God has never made me feel small or worthless.

One of my favorite Bible verses suddenly popped into my mind: "The Word became flesh and made his dwelling among us. We have seen his glory, the glory of the one and only Son, who came from the Father, *full of grace and truth*" (John 1:14, italics mine).

Perhaps those words speak so powerfully to me because each day I am aware of needing and receiving "grace in place of grace already given" (John 1:16).

"Grace in place of grace"—like an overflowing fountain bringing forgiveness and hope instead of humiliation.

Now if that doesn't take your breath away, you may not be breathing.

# Runaway Walker

On my last visit with my sister, I was startled when she said, "I lost my walker last Tuesday."

"Honey," I replied, "I know how difficult it is for you to walk, but if your walker walked off and left you, maybe you ought to pick it up just a little."

Ginny lives alone in the little town of Albemarle, North Carolina, since my brother-in-law's death a few years earlier. Bill and Ginny were married for more than fifty-five years before his chronic heart problems—which he successfully fought for many years—finally overcame him. Theirs was a love affair that began when Ginny was still in high school. She was a very studious, bright student and would have done extremely well in college, but they were eager to begin their life together, so Ginny began working in the bank in Mt. Gilead to earn money for their upcoming wedding in December 1957. That marriage produced three outstanding children, Eric, Lisa, and Kevin; six delightful grandchildren; and one very special great-grandchild.

I have great admiration for my sister, who keeps moving, refusing to be a victim of severe rheumatoid arthritis and all the other illnesses that usually accompany that affliction. Ginny lets none of that keep her from church, shopping, getting her hair done, visiting nursing homes, and going out to eat with family even though it would be easier and much less painful to stay home and curl up with a good book or ballgame.

True to form, Ginny was on her way to a birthday party at a local nursing home when her walker disappeared. A friend, Margaret Radford, had picked her up and carefully placed the walker in the back of her Chevrolet SUV. Halfway to their destination, however, Ginny looked back and was startled to see her walker was mysteriously missing.

Margaret couldn't believe it when she pulled over and opened the hatch door to find nothing but an empty space. With tear-filled eyes she said, "Ginny, I guess I'll have to buy you a new walker."

"You'll have to buy me more than that, Margaret," my sister replied. "My cellphone and wallet and all my credit cards were in a pocket on the front of the walker."

That began an hour of frantic activity, starting with retracing the trip and calling in family members and friends to help. After all, the little hamlet of Albemarle is not that large. There were just so many places a runaway walker could hide.

Finally, they called 911. The woman told them to stay where they were and she would dispatch a patrol car. Folks in small towns take care of each other.

Very soon, much to my sister's embarrassment, the word was out all over town about the walker, which did not just run away but leaped out of the back of a Chevrolet SUV when the unlocked door popped up just enough for the impatient walker to see a slight opening.

Thankfully, before the patrol car arrived, the 911 operator called back with the happy news that a woman had found the walker in the middle of a street and rescued it at some risk to her own life. She had turned it in at the police station downtown, where Ginny and Margaret rushed to retrieve it with much relief.

Parking out front, the two friends sat for a few moments, reflecting over the frantic events before my sister finally said, "Margaret, you're going to have to go get it. I can't walk without my walker."

Everyone in town was overjoyed that the mystery of the runaway walker had been solved and things could return to normal. But I felt I should give my sister a warning: "If you see your walker getting restless again, Ginny, you might need to trade it in for an older model that appreciates a slower pace. Or, like I said, you might need to pick it up a little."

I thought that was funny and started laughing. Thankfully, my sister has a great sense of humor and began laughing along with me.

Actually, all of this was reminding me of one of my favorite verses in all of Scripture: "But those who hope in the Lord will renew their strength. They will soar on wings like eagles; they will run and not grow weary, they will walk and not be faint." (Isa 40:31).

"Waiting for the Lord" paints a picture for me of looking upward toward God rather than down and around at the things that are happening in my present life.

Sometimes life shoots us down and grounds us and forces us to move at a snail's pace. The trick is to have the determination and the faith to find a way to keep moving.

Ginny suffered a fall recently, which has made it necessary for her to leave her home and move to a facility where she has assistance in caring for her daily needs. Walking has become even more difficult.

But mounting up on wings like eagles and running and walking are still possibilities if we wait on God—a God who looks beyond physical limitations to the heart and the spirit. In the realm of the spiritual, there are no restrictions to movement.

In fact, I have confidence that, each day, Ginny—like all of us on the Mullinix journey—can discover new ways to "pick it up a little" as we "wait for the Lord."

# Skinny Doctor

I once had a skinny doctor. She was so slender that I worried about her.

I remember my mother saying that everyone ought to carry around a few extra pounds in case one gets sick and starts losing weight. "Without a good supply of fat to burn, a person could waste away to nothin' in no time at all," my mother would say.

My very skinny doctor had not even an ounce of excess fat to burn and, according to my mother, was in constant danger of wasting away to nothing. That would have been a shame because I liked her a lot. She would actually sit and talk to me as if my health really mattered to her on a personal, rather than merely a professional, level.

On my last visit, just prior to her taking another position in order to spend more time with her family, I asked her what she had eaten for breakfast. It was an early morning appointment, and she looked hungry. Also, breakfast is my favorite meal, and I like for people to enjoy it as much as I do.

My doctor's puzzled frown told me she thought it was a curious question. But, like I said, she's always willing to talk and proceeded to tell me she had eaten one half cup of reduced-fat yogurt, three orange slices, and four pitted prunes along with a small glass of skim milk.

I took a deep breath to repress the gag reflex pushing bitter bile up my throat. Gaining control over the sudden reflux, I asked if she had ever tried three lightly scrambled eggs mixed with a little whole milk or maybe with a tablespoon of water if you like maximum fluffiness.

Before my skinny doctor could answer, I hurried on, "Of course you need to complement those eggs with two strips of crisp bacon and a large patty of hot sausage, paired with a big bowl of heavily buttered grits, carefully seasoned with just the right amount of salt and pepper. And don't forget three or four homemade lard biscuits and a generous portion of fig preserves, also homemade, to finish off that last biscuit."

Noticing that she had already progressed through several shades of green, I didn't mention one of my other favorites—thin slices of pungent liver pudding carefully fried so that the outside is crispy while preserving the tasty mushiness inside.

My skinny doctor pressed so hard against her abdomen—dealing with her own reflux problem, I suppose—that I was fearful she might break a rib—unprotected as her rib cage was by even a thin layer of fat.

After settling her unruly, though tiny stomach, my skinny doctor looked up with pained eyes and said, "You know, I haven't said much about your weight recently." I told her how grateful I was for that and what a compassionate friend she was. But she quickly continued, "Do you think maybe you *could* lose five pounds before I see you again in six months?"

"Five pounds shouldn't be a problem," I replied cheerfully, relieved that she hadn't said fifty. Thinking I'd better not push my luck, I chose not to suggest any more breakfast menus even though I remained seriously concerned about her lack of weight. Well, she's a doctor, so maybe if she gets sick, she can write a prescription for herself to reverse the whole process before she "wastes away to nothin'."

In the meantime, I remain secure in my response to my wife's suggestions of a new diet: "But just think," I say, recalling Mother's words, "if I become ill, I'm way ahead of the game." Jean takes an optimistic view of most things, but my efforts to characterize extra pounds as a blessing have never impressed her, even when I bring the Apostle Paul into the argument.

I've always felt Paul was the supreme authority on the subject of how "bad" things can become "good" things. After all, he had certainly experienced his share of such transformations.

For instance, Paul had prayed repeatedly for God to remove the "thorn" that tormented him. "But [the Lord] said to [Paul], 'My grace is sufficient for you, for my power is made perfect in weakness'.... That is why, for Christ's sake, I delight in weaknesses, in insults, in hardships, in persecutions, in difficulties. For when I am weak, then I am strong." (2 Cor 12:9, 10b). The perfect example of the seemingly bad turned into a good.

I've experienced that in my own life when, as much as it frustrates and irritates me and as much as I've tried to change it, my soul seems to stretch more in the bad times than in the good times. I'd much prefer to do my best growing in good times and forget about the suffering. But I just can't seem to pull it off.

During the hard miles on the way to Mullinix, I try to remain patient and watchful to see how God is going to use even my pain—or maybe *especially* my pain—to lift me to the next level of kingdom living.

I still worry about my exceptionally slender doctor, however, and can't help thinking it's a bad thing to be that skinny. But as my exam was concluded, I was reminded of the blessings of the skinny fingers.

Right again, Paul.

# Musical Misfit

While exiting from our morning worship service, the smiling William & Mary student paused long enough to say, "Did you know you sound like Burl Ives?"

I returned his smile and said, "Some people seem to think so." Then I added my customary response: "Just wish I could sing like Burl."

Over the years, many people have said words similar to this college student. I used to wonder how students even knew Burl Ives since he died in 1995 and his most active singing and acting career took place much earlier.

I stopped wondering when a student reminded me that Ives was the voice of Sam the Snowman in the cartoon movie *Rudolph the Red-Nosed Reindeer*. Then, of course, Burl made the song of the same name popular before one of my boyhood cowboy heroes, Gene Autrey, got hold of it.

So I no longer ask college students how they know Burl Ives, one of the greatest folk singers and balladeers of all time. But I still say truthfully, "I promise you I don't sound at all like him when I sing."

I don't bother to explain that I am a musical misfit in a family of musicians. My mother and father both sang in the church choir with Daddy leading the choir on occasion. My older sister, Ginny, began accompanying the choir and a church quartet on the piano when she was twelve. My younger sister, Donna, still accompanies her church choir on the piano and/or organ while also directing. And, of course, my brother Kent has sung solos along with participating in other singing groups. He also has had stints of directing church choirs.

Which leaves me having to be content, albeit somewhat envious, to watch and enjoy their gifts. In all honesty, I have no choice.

A good example of that is the summer my wife talked me into singing a duet with her during a women's retreat at Eastover Plantation in Surry, Virginia, many years ago. Predictably, we had to quit halfway through the second verse because Jean was laughing so hard that she could not continue.

In between hysterical fits of laughter, I understood her to say something about me changing keys so often that she couldn't keep up. Jean had no answer when I asked her how I could change keys when I didn't even know what a key was.

Needless to say, that was the end of my misguided attempts to sing—publicly or privately. Well, I do try to sing along with Johnny Cash occasionally when I'm alone in the car. Thought it might be worth a try since I heard some unkind soul tell a laughing audience that Johnny even talked off key.

I wondered if he, like me, could also cry off key.

I was twelve years old when we brought my younger sister, Donna, home from the hospital. There was such a crowded houseful of people waiting to see this new addition to our family that we were delayed in preparing her bottle. Her hungry wails were disturbing to my twelve-year-old uninitiated ears, but Mother said calmly, "Don't worry. It's a very natural thing. Babies cry to let us know they need something."

When the bottle was finally sterilized and my sister could no longer howl because her mouth was full of milk, Mother continued, "Crying babies never bothered me."

As I sat and watched Donna hungrily devour the milk, Mother expounded a little more on crying babies. Looking up at me, she smiled and said, "Jerry, your crying was a little different."

"Really?"

"It was strange. You seemed to cry a little off key."

Mother later vehemently insisted, "Jerry, I never said anything of the sort!" I would laughingly admit that things were a little hectic around the house that day, so I could be wrong, but that's the way I remembered it.

Besides, I feel like I have a very valid excuse when it comes to my lack of musical ability. I was born in a little frame house on E. Allenton St. in downtown Mt. Gilead, North Carolina. Many times, I can remember Mother telling me (she didn't deny saying this) that when the doctor sat on the edge of the bed to assist her in the delivery, the wooden slats gave way, and the entire bed collapsed to the floor with a loud bang.

The way I figure it, not only did I begin life at a very low point with a long way to climb up, but I also have a suspicion that when I hit the floor, my tender newborn vocal chords suffered irreparable damage. In fact, I think I may have experienced a "concussion of the vocal chords." Back on October 19, 1940, they had no protocol to diagnose and treat such things. Incredibly, it took seventy-five years to set up a protocol for concussed football players, so I guess my tiny vocal chords never had a chance to be diagnosed and treated.

As a result, years later, when Donna joined Ginny at the piano in our living room as all the family gathered around to sing Christmas carols, Donna would say softly over her shoulder, "Somebody's gotta drop out." No one doubted who that "somebody" was. Donna also vehemently denies that she ever said such a thing. It is absolutely astounding to me that two intelligent women like my mother and younger sister could have such poor memories. It does, however, cause me to wonder if my usually reliable, keen memory is fallible after all. Or is my memory subject to outside influences that have distorted it?

I've seen it happen. Many church squabbles have resulted from unreliable memories that have twisted the actual words of another.

Many times, when I've tried to get at the source of a controversy, I've heard words similar to my mother's and sister's: "I said no such thing!"

Is it possible that I imagined those words because I felt I deserved such an evaluation of my musical ability?

It's kind of breathtaking to realize the power of our fallible memories to distort reality.

I have long ago made peace with my lack of musical ability. In his letter to the Romans, Paul makes it very clear that we are not supposed to have the same gifts: "For just as each of us has one body with many members, and these members do not all have the same function, we have different gifts, according to the grace given to each of us" (Rom 12:4, 6).

Along the way, I have learned to be content with the grace gifts given to me. Besides, if I can't sing like Burl Ives, sounding a little like him is not a bad substitute.

# Remembering Poopsie

A constant parade of people pass our home on Jameswood in First Colony. By the way, it's just "Jameswood"—no "Road," "Street," "Avenue," or any similar suffix—in spite of those frustrated people who insist on adding one or more of the above. It's just "Jameswood"; we must all learn to live with it.

I know very few of the strolling neighbors by name, but I have learned to identify many of them by their pets. The other day, however, a pet was missing. After a brief conversation, I wondered if perhaps the dog's owner was also missing—at least partially.

Late one afternoon, a middle-aged woman I had not seen for a long time was walking by just as I had seated myself comfortably in my favorite white slated rocking chair on our expansive front porch. From this chair, I often watch the sun drop behind the trees separating our house from the James River, a quarter of a mile to the west. Occasionally, I slip into the twilight zone of a light slumber.

Approximately a hundred feet of a sparse green and brown lawn separates our front porch from the street. With a number of large trees surrounding our yard and house, it's impossible to have a plush lawn. But I've always loved trees.

On this late afternoon, however, I thought my eyes were deceiving me. Maybe it was finally time to have that cataract/cornea surgery. I could see the leash but not the dog. It didn't take me long to realize the woman was holding one of those trick leashes that extends forward on its own. They've been around so long that they no longer hold any interest for me—not even eliciting a smile.

However, on this occasion, in addition to the leash, I noticed a suspicious-looking dark gray plastic bag in the woman's left hand.

Now that, too, is a familiar sight since most folks are conscientious about picking up the waste their dogs deposit along the road, often on the edges of plush lawns and, most popularly, beside mailboxes. My mailbox, which I have recently painted the colors of my alma mater, the University of North Carolina in Chapel Hill, seemed to be the favorite place for pets to leave their calling cards for friends and strangers alike. At least, I hoped they were leaving messages for other canines rather than commenting on my beloved school.

In the years we've lived on Jameswood since building our house in 1987, I've seen some unusual things pass along the road without giving them much attention. But I could not ignore this curious scene of a woman carrying a bag full of dog poop with no dog at the end of her leash.

Reluctantly rising from my chair and walking briskly to the edge of the road, I called out a cheerful "Good afternoon!"

"Hi," she replied with a big smile.

"I don't mean to disturb your walk," I continued, "but I couldn't help but notice that you have no dog but appear to have a bag filled with dog poop."

Her head nodded up and down enthusiastically. "You're very observant. Most people don't seem to question it." I wasn't surprised at that since I had learned long ago that most people don't pay much attention to what's going on around them.

We just don't notice.

One Sunday afternoon, a man who had attended worship that morning with his teenage daughter called to tell me what she had said on the way home: "Daddy, do you think all those stories really happen to Pastor Haywood, or does he make them up?" I could tell by his questioning tone that he was wondering the same thing.

"Tell her," I said, "that, yes, they really do happen, and they will happen to her if she just pays attention."

"You are the first person to question me about this bag," the woman repeated, still sounding surprised. Holding up the plastic bag, she told her story: "This is all I have left of Poopsie."

"Poopsie?" I thought to myself. She has to be putting me on. But I replied, "That's kind of an unusual name for a dog."

"Yes, it is," she replied. "It's actually a nickname she earned by a behavioral characteristic like some of those Old Testament characters I've studied in Sunday school." Most folks in the neighborhood knew I was a retired pastor and often liked to slip in biblical references whenever possible. I was never sure whether they wanted to impress themselves or me or God.

"You know," she continued, warming to her theological discourse, "like Jacob, who wrestled with God. So his God-given name was 'Israel,' which means 'struggles with God.'" She paused momentarily, gazing at me smugly, trying to gauge how deeply she had impressed me.

I smiled and nodded slightly. "Wow! You must have really been paying attention in church last Sunday."

Pleased with my reaction, my neighbor continued, "Her real name was Penelope Jane Smith. She was a very unusual French poodle. A teacup poodle. She never ate much, but when we went for a walk, she would stop every fifty feet to leave a deposit. I never could bring enough plastic bags to keep up with her generosity."

My curiosity was growing with each new revelation. "When did she die?" I asked.

"Two years ago," Poopsie's owner replied quickly, seemingly wanting to talk, as I know most folks who have suffered a loss do. "She lived to be sixteen-and-a-half years old and was still black as soot when she died—just a few gray hairs around her mouth and nose. Small dogs live longer than big dogs, you know. But she finally went deaf and blind and lost control of her bowels."

"How could you tell?" I interrupted irreverently. Hardly noticing my weak attempt at humor (see what I mean about folks not noticing), she finished by saying, "But then she started having seizures, and we had to put her down." Little pools of unshed tears began collecting in the corners of each eye.

"I'm glad you were able to enjoy her so long," I said, trying to turn the conversation in a more positive direction. Experience has taught me that such attempts are most often useless in times of grief. This time, however, it seemed to work.

"I'm *still* enjoying her," she said, her smile returning as she raised the plastic bag higher.

"Is that really…?" I stammered.

"Yep," she said, nodding with satisfaction. "I saved this bag of Poopsie's poop so that she would always be with me."

I had read many years ago, in researching a sermon, that smell is the sense most closely connected to the area of the brain having to do with memory and emotions, so I could understand something of this neighbor's thinking.

I thought briefly of how woodsmoke on a chilly fall day would transport me back to my North Carolina boyhood, when smoke rising from every chimney on every house filled the air with the aroma of the many varieties of wood used by our family and surrounding neighbors in their fireplaces and wood-burning cook stoves.

My neighbor quickly brought me back to the present when she concluded, "Every time I catch a whiff of this poop, it's as if Poopsie is walking the neighborhood with me again. I find it very comforting."

As I told her goodbye and walked back across the yard toward our front porch, my mind was busily processing this strange encounter. Memory is a powerful thing and can carry us in many directions. It can just as easily bring us sadness as well as joy and comfort.

I met a young woman at a local restaurant's salad bar recently. She was watching me spoon some New England clam chowder into my paper bowl. "I can't eat New England clam chowder anymore," she said. I could hear the sadness in her voice.

I paused in my spooning and turned to her, my curiosity stirred. "Oh?" I inquired eloquently.

"My grandfather died last year," she said. "We were very close." I stood facing her with my tray and the half-filled bowl of clam chowder in my left hand while holding the dipping spoon in my right, waiting for her to continue.

"Certain aromas remind me of him. New England clam chowder is one of them." She was tearing up as she continued, "And hot chocolate and Old Spice aftershave lotion." Reaching up with her left hand, she wiped her eyes with a napkin. "Those things just make my memory too intense."

We were strangers, and I was a little surprised at how easily she shared her feelings. Maybe I reminded her of her grandfather. But she was finished now, and we stood facing each other in an awkward silence.

I looked down at my paper bowl half-filled with clam chowder and asked, "Should I pour it back?"

She laughed and said, "No, go ahead and eat it. Just sit over in the corner so I can't smell it."

We said goodbye—strangers who had immediately become fellow pilgrims—as I filled the bowl and walked toward a far corner. The New England clam chowder was good, but once again I was thinking more about the power of memory than I was of the chowder.

In the fourth chapter of Joshua, Joshua called together twelve men he had appointed, one from each of the Israelite tribes, and told them to pile up stones from the middle of the Jordan River. Then, when their children asked "What do these stones mean?," they could tell them that they were a memorial, a reminder of God's faithfulness in cutting off the flow of the Jordan so the people could follow the priests carrying the ark of the covenant across the river (Josh 4:6–7).

When fighting off cynicism and despair and bitterness in a world full of confusion, corruption, and exploitation of all kinds, I recognize my own need for those symbols that help me remember God is faithful. We all have a need for those memorials, which, as Paul said "stir up our memories."

As I walked back to the front porch, random thoughts raced through my mind. For one thing, how did my neighbor sustain the aroma of Poopsie's poop for so long? Might contain the secret of keeping food fresh longer. I also thought of the shoes and pacifiers my wife had saved from our children's baby years and idly wondered if maybe we could have done more to preserve the memories of their young years.

One more thought suddenly struck me as I plopped onto my comfortable rocker: "Had I just been pranked?" Something wasn't quite right about this whole episode.

I squinted through the bushes and trees, trying to catch a final glimpse of Poopsie's owner as she walked leisurely down Jameswood toward John Rolfe—the main road leading into First Colony. My neighbor still held the empty leash in one hand and the two-year-old bag of dog poop in the other.

Were those shimmering heatwaves playing tricks on my eyes, or were her shoulders shaking slightly from suppressed laughter?

A few minutes later, as I stretched and stood to seek the cooler, air-conditioned indoors, I noticed that my legs were sore and stiff, giving rise to another disquieting thought: "Had I dozed off and dreamed the whole thing?"

At least the entire experience was an important reminder. In moving toward the completion of my unfinished story of redemption, I need to hang on to as many pieces of memory as possible—especially those memories of people and places and events that have left me breathless with richness, healing, hope, and continuing faith in a good God.

It was also a reminder that memory doesn't always require a large pile of stones.

# Part Three

A Breathtaking Journey

Is Touched by Lives Well Lived

# A Life That Took My Breath Away

Audrey Kay Page Watson drew her last breath on November 29, 2017. But all her life, Audrey had been taking my breath away.

We celebrated her amazing life in a service on the first Sunday of Advent, December 3, 2017. Even with a heavy heart, I could not help thinking, "What better time could a person like Audrey Kay pass from this life into her next than in the season of Advent."

It was such a fitting time for someone who lived an Advent life—a life full to running over with hope, peace, joy, and love.

Audrey Kay began life in a scary darkness that cried out for the light. On October 6, 1978, shortly after entering this world, Audrey Kay's mother, Glenda, called us with some hard news. In addition to cystic fibrosis, the pretty, dark-haired little girl was born with other severe physical problems that required immediate abdominal surgery with lasting health challenges.

The doctors told her parents that Audrey Kay would probably not live long enough to go home with them. But with Advent hope, Glenda and Joe said they believed God might write another ending to that story.

That hope, exemplified in her parents, stayed with Audrey Kay throughout her life. Not only did she come home from the hospital, but Audrey kept confounding the medical community with her will not merely to live but to thrive and accomplish.

With an indomitable hope and determination, the little girl who was not expected to live long enough to make it home finished college at Longwood in less than four years. All of this was accomplished in spite of bouts of illness that required numerous trips to the hospital for the treatments needed to set her on her way again.

Audrey always was "on the way" with places to go that no one ever thought she could reach—or should even attempt. But hope—resting on a solid foundation of faith—drew her on.

When she graduated from college, she went to work immediately for James City County in a temporary job. Well, it was temporary until they discovered who Audrey Kay was as a person and as an employee. They then felt compelled to create a permanent job, which she held for almost eighteen years, serving as president of many professional organizations along the way.

Audrey Kay continually changed lives and situations by the strength of a heart and soul filled with Advent hope. So on that first Sunday—the day of Audrey Kay's funeral—we lit the candle of hope.

It was all so fitting that I sometimes found it hard to breathe as I gave her eulogy.

The candle of peace would be lit the next Sunday. The church calendar said that was the way it was supposed to be. But Audrey Kay never waited for special seasons or days to bring to full flame the candle of peace. Her very presence, each moment and each day, radiated peace—even when she was struggling to breathe and her attempts at a deep breath would bring on spasms of coughing.

We all held our breath in awe.

But really we knew the source of such peace. Her peace did not depend on Audrey's ability to breathe but in being surrounded by the breath of God.

She wrote a continuing blog, "Breathing with Audrey," that was more substantive than many devotional books I've come across. Here's a portion of one blog written October 14, 2013:

God's hugs are always on time. I have felt this over and over and over again through this journey especially [Audrey is speaking of her torturous journey of a double lung transplant at Duke University]. This journey and the process that the hospital aggressively puts you through is something I could never have imagined.... I find myself constantly calling on the Lord to just hold me.... I have made it a habit to receive a hug multiple times a day from my Lord, and I have noticed that sometimes I can feel the hugs when I haven't even asked! God is good.

That's what biblical peace is all about. And it comes through the kind of trust that enables us to receive God's generous gifts of grace through continuous hugs. Audrey's kind of peace is not something we attain but is a gift that assures us that safety and security are our eternal possessions.

Near the end of his earthly ministry, Jesus promised his disciples, "'Peace I leave with you; my peace I give you. I do not give to you as the world gives. Do not let your hearts be troubled and do not be afraid'" (John 14:27).

Audrey Kay not only embraced that promise but freely shared her secret—open arms to receive God's encircling hugs every minute of the day.

Oh, the unfathomable joy. On our refrigerator—along with the pictures of children and grandchildren and granddogs and wedding invitations—we have a large picture of Audrey with her signature beatific smile. It brings me joy every time I see it.

It's easy to see why Audrey's favorite flower was the sunflower. I heard someone say that no flower lifts the spirit quite so much as a sunflower. So bright, cheery, warm, and inviting—no wonder it's often called the "happy" flower.

Audrey was the incarnation of all the qualities of the sunflower—a living, breathing, walking sunflower—bigger than life!

How could Audrey Kay radiate such joy in the middle of intense struggle and pain—even beyond our ability to imagine?

Karl Booth wrote one time that "joy is the simplest form of gratitude." In her gratitude for God's hugs of love, and the fact that in spite of her illness, she was given a chance at life, joy flooded Audrey Kay's very being. And it was highly contagious—infecting those who were in contact with her for just a brief moment or those who have found a permanent place for that smile on the refrigerator.

Audrey's joyful gratitude certainly was also due to the unconditional love and loyalty she received from her mother, Glenda, and her husband, Zach. Glenda, who was always by Audrey's side through all the highs and lows, told me on one occasion, "Zach's thoughts and actions have always been directed toward Audrey before himself and his own desires." When Glenda would have them over for dinner, she would ask Zach what he wanted and he would always reply, "Whatever Audrey's having."

In my world, for a man to say he will eat whatever his wife is eating—no matter what it is—is pure, unadulterated, unselfish love.

That's also the kind of love that completes the Advent wreath and brings God's "hugs" full circle.

In an article in the 2013 Advent booklet that our minister of education, Linda Ward, so capably edited each year, Audrey wrote,

> God not only was with me on this journey of lung transplantation, but he saw fit to continually be my strength when I was too weak, and my hope when I felt there was none. He did this through so many "ordinary miracles" each and every day over the past five months.... As an ordinary person, I have once again experienced God's miracle. I'm alive. I can breathe. My lung capacity which was at 14 percent prior to my transplant is now 80 percent and continuing to improve. To breathe with such ease for the first time in 35 years is truly a miracle!

Three wonderful years of deep breaths followed her lung transplant. In summer 2016 when I was leading a prayer service at Walnut Hills, we sang "Happy Birthday" to mark the third anniversary of Audrey Kay's new lungs. She was without doubt "born again," as she was able to breathe without restriction or coughing for the first time in her life.

But a few months later, complications began to develop, and Audrey Kay returned to Duke Hospital in a very weakened condition. Her devoted husband and mother, of course, remained by her side.

Zach told me about a time in the hospital when Audrey was taking the required laps in the hallways when she passed a man who had undergone a heart-lung transplant and was struggling greatly to continue his prescribed laps—collapsing onto the seat attached to his walker every two or three steps.

Pausing before him, Audrey Kay said, "I've been there, just where you are, and I promise you it will get better." Even in the middle of her own severe struggles, Audrey's deep love for God spilled over in compassion and unmeasured empathy for all suffering humanity.

Those words lifted the man off his walker to take a few more laborious steps. Each time Audrey Kay passed, she would smile that smile, which spoke so much hope, peace, joy, and love to a broken, hurting world.

It's easy to understand why Audrey Kay's favorite quote was one by Hilary Cooper: "Life is not measured by the number of breaths we take, but by the moments that take our breath away."

I thank God for breathtaking "moments" along the journey to Mullinix—that place where we experience the presence of God in as much fullness as we can know in this world.

*Individual* moments, however, are one thing. To experience an entire *life* that takes my breath away is far greater.

Thank you, Audrey Kay, for the gift of a life with the power to lift me out of dark valleys and send me on my way again—on the way toward those divine arms waiting to embrace me, as they do you now, in an *eternal hug*.

After Christmas, Audrey, we blew out the candles on the Advent wreath. But the candles you lit will never be extinguished.

# Heart Trouble?

I was playing hide-and-seek with my brother Kent and two of my Asheboro cousins, Darryl and David Garner, when the floor suddenly collapsed beneath my right foot.

I quickly discovered that what I thought was an attic floor was in reality the backside of a brand-new living room ceiling. Now it was a new ceiling with a huge hole through which my leg was dangling precariously as I desperately held on to the crossbeams with both arms.

Glancing through the hole with terrified eyes, I had a clear picture of my Uncle Vernon with all kinds of debris raining down upon him as he stood looking upward with arms outstretched. I still wonder at his presence of mind to attempt to catch whomever or whatever might be coming through the hole in his ceiling. It isn't every day that your ceiling collapses on your head.

Standing next to Uncle Vernon were my parents. Ceiling tiles were the latest thing back then, and Uncle Vernon had been explaining the virtues of such a ceiling, which he and his wife, my daddy's sister Evelyn, had just installed.

I had glanced at the ceiling earlier as we hurriedly passed through the living room on the way to our game of hide-and-seek. Now, I was mortified that I had suddenly and riotously punched a large gaping hole in that lovely new addition to their home.

The walk from the attic to the living room was one of the longest walks of my young life. In those moments, I felt that I understood a little of what it was like to take that prisoner's walk from death row to the execution chamber. But they at least had a minister walking beside them—praying all the way with an open Bible in his hands. I only had a brother and two first cousins, all younger than me, who were just as frightened—albeit much more innocent, guilty only by association with their delinquent playmate.

Embarrassment, guilt, humiliation, dread—more emotions than I could identify at that age—weighed down upon me as I dragged my reluctant feet down the steps to face the judgment I was certain awaited me.

Much to my surprise, however, I learned something about God that day from my Uncle Vernon. In place of the anger and condemnation I had expected, Uncle Vernon looked at me with sympathy and understanding. He sensed how I felt and extended a large portion of unexpected kindness, which could only be explained by grace—undeserved love and forgiveness.

I had always admired his quiet, gentle nature, but even at that young age, his response to my destructive deed struck me as a remarkable example of valuing the needs of people over things. As I watched Uncle Vernon complete the task of brushing the bits of tile and asbestos from his hair, he kept watching me with understanding eyes and a warm smile.

When my daddy—naturally embarrassed for me—told Uncle Vernon he would pay for the repairs, Uncle Vernon shook his head in protest. "Oh no, that won't be necessary," he said. "I'll just call the man on Monday, and he'll come staple a few pieces back up there. Take just a few minutes."

Even as a young boy, I knew the job of restoring the ceiling to its original state was not going to be that simple. But those few words, dramatically downplaying the extent of my transgression, have shaped me in more ways than I can imagine.

For instance, many years later, as I became familiar with Paul's list of the fruit of the Spirit—love, joy, peace, patience, kindness, generosity, faithfulness, gentleness, and self-control (Gal 5:22–23a)—I probably understood them better than most. Those qualities were easy for me to visualize. I had seen them demonstrated before my frightened, humiliated eyes as a young boy.

Over the years, I have tried hard to follow my Uncle Vernon's example of holding my arms wide to catch those poor, careless souls who have tumbled through a variety of holes in numerous ceilings—holes often, like mine, of their own making.

Years later, in 1960, while still a college student, I was saddened to hear that Uncle Vernon had suffered a heart attack. The first heart bypass surgery took place in May of that same year, but such surgeries were not commonly practiced until many years later.

I remember traveling to the Medical College of Virginia in Richmond in the early 1970s with a parishioner needing a bypass. The family and I arrived before dawn and were still awaiting the completion of the surgery after sunset. Even then, the outcome was in question, and recovery was long and difficult.

Uncle Vernon lived a relatively normal life for a number of years following his first heart attack. But by 1983 his heart had deteriorated to the point that doctors felt a triple bypass was needed. Bypasses were now becoming more common and safer.

However, I learned recently that Uncle Vernon experienced a premonition, telling his wife, "If they decide to do surgery, I don't think I'll survive."

It was devastating, therefore, when a phone call informed me that Uncle Vernon's premonition was correct. He had passed away on the operating table. The surgery seemed to be a success, but they could not restart Uncle Vernon's heart.

My first thought was, "That's impossible!" Uncle Vernon's heart never had a problem getting started. Especially at the sight of a frightened little boy who didn't even know enough to keep his foot out of an expensive new ceiling.

But life is full of such painful ironies. Thank God life is also full of people like Uncle Vernon. These are the ones who pave the way for others to become what our Lord has called us all to be—living vessels empowered to receive God's grace and then pass it on to others. The very thought of that possibility is enough to cause a catch in my usually normal, rhythmic breathing.

# Tripping or Journeying?

He burst into my office without a knock or a greeting. Plunging immediately into his purpose for stopping by, he said loudly, "Pastor, you won't see me and my wife for a while. Headin' home to Texas!"

Smiling as I tried to recover from the boisterous interruption, I said, "Well, I hope you have a good trip."

"We will," he replied enthusiastically. "Plan to beat the travel time of our last trip, even though it was a record." I remembered. His wife had told me she had seriously considered divorce as her husband raced by rest stop after rest stop—only pausing briefly at welcome centers when they crossed state lines.

His wife knew there was more than one way to take a trip. This wasn't her way.

Neither was it Wanda Sublett's.

The second snowstorm had followed quickly—much too soon for the first one to even partially be cleared. Headlines in the *Virginia Gazette* were mostly about everyone grousing about the weather; "Misery Accumulates" was the lead story on the front page. Not only were people running out of groceries, but children could not attend school, and parents could not get to work.

When I turned to the sports section, I read at the top of the first page, "Snow's Woes Accumulate"—referring to the necessity of confusing schedule changes for all the ballgames. Cabin fever was rampant, and family conflicts were rising to a danger point.

Except in the Sublett home.

Over in the letter section of that same *Gazette* was another headline—"Blizzard Blessings." In the letter, a lady named Wanda Sublett wrote:

The third snowstorm has come and gone. My three daughters have missed many days from school because of the snow, but the blessings of their presence at home are treasured. I teach part-time, and I was able to be at home with them reading stories, working puzzles, sledding, drinking hot chocolate, baking cookies, laughing, sharing, snuggling under warm afghans to watch several special videos—moments to remember. The children are now back in school. Maybe the predicted March snowstorm will give me one more opportunity to share special moments of parenthood. Time goes too quickly. (February 25, 1996)

Many people were amazed at such an attitude since all they had heard for many days was loud, high-pitched complaining and whining.

But I was not in the least surprised. Wanda Sublett always had a way of looking at life and describing what she was seeing in a manner that was all her own. She and her husband, Tom, and their three daughters, Kim, Whitney, and Melanie, had been members of our church for many years—Wanda and Tom prior to the birth of their children.

Not only were they church members, but all were special friends. Wanda was also a colleague, serving as our volunteer youth minister for six years in the late 1970s and early 1980s. Tom held many positions but felt that one of his most important jobs was to keep me humble by noting slips of the tongue or brain during my sermons. One Sunday, he handed me an odd-looking piece of sports equipment. Puzzled, I looked at him and asked, "What's this?"

"Well," Tom deadpanned, "since you talked about a 'golf racket' in last Sunday's sermon, I thought I would make one for you."

So there it was—the shaft of a golf club attached snugly to a badminton racket head.

I always thought humility was one of my strengths. In fact, I was always kind of proud of how humble I could be. But Tom felt my humility could use some help, so who was I to argue? That "golf racket" still hangs in our garage as a lasting symbol of my many imperfections.

It was things like this that caused Wanda to feel it necessary to come to me one day and try to explain Tom. "Jer, you know he's a great guy. He does crazy…"

Raising my hand quickly, I said, "Wanda, stop right there. I know Tom. I know his heart. I love him like a brother."

Visibly relaxing, Wanda started laughing. "Isn't he a piece of work?"

Where young people were involved, my wife, Jean, was always there to assist Wanda—especially on youth retreats. As concerned husbands, Tom and I would show up at some of those retreats. We were like nervous fathers—trying to protect the youth by corralling them and keeping them on short leashes.

Wanda and Jean did not believe in short or long leashes. Felt they were unnecessary. Their only leash was *trust*—trust that the youth would respect them enough to follow safety instructions.

One weekend, while teetering on the edge of a nervous breakdown as the youth were scattering in all directions, I began to understand the wisdom of this. They wanted the youth to throw themselves into the retreat. Experience the moment fully—which was the way Wanda lived her life.

Wanda would often sit in my church study following youth conferences and tell me about her experiences. She was always genuinely surprised when the first thing other youth ministers asked about was her salary. Laughing, she would tell them "I make exactly zero dollars annually." Telling that story would bring on an episode of her infectious, deep-throated chuckling.

At that point in our church's life, we could not afford multiple paid staff personnel. But Wanda loved the youth far too much to let that stop her.

As I have reflected on those years, I have come to see those youth retreats as microcosms of Wanda's life. There are always risks, but the only way to have a full life lies in understanding all the pieces—even a crippling blizzard—as a *journey* to be experienced rather than a hurried *trip* to reach a destination.

The clues were all around her busy life. For instance, Wanda was always late—refusing to be hurried. Why rush through the important moments of life? Moments that may never be replicated. Moments that might run out too soon.

"Time goes too quickly."

Her unique style of conversation was another clue to her worldview. When Wanda would stop me in the hall and say she wanted to talk, I knew I was in for a treat. I would invite her into my study, where I could sit in a soft chair and get comfortable for the journey I knew was coming.

As Wanda's words painted one scene after another, I began a little mind game. "Now, let's see. I believe this is what we're talking about. No. Wait a minute. Here comes another bend in the road. Hang on, Jerry. The journey is just beginning."

Suddenly, Wanda would pause and ask anxiously, "Do you see where I'm going, Jer?"

"I will, Wanda, I will. Keep going."

And so the journey continued as my anticipation grew until Wanda finally concluded, "So this is what I think is the best thing to do." Then, after carefully presenting her destination/conclusion, she would ask, "What do you think?"

Well, Wanda had carried me along the journey of her thought processes so thoroughly—painting a picture at each stop along the way—that by the time we arrived, I was completely convinced.

To be true to Wanda's personality, however, I must confess that not everyone could follow her free-wheeling stream of thought as easily as I. Carol Bynum, the longtime director of the Walnut Hills Learning Center where Wanda taught the "Little Monkeys" class, was telling me of many parents' reactions following a meeting with Wanda in one of their periodic parent/teacher conferences.

Walking slowly down the hall, they would be shaking their heads and with a puzzled frown say, "I'm not sure what she said, but I think it was all good."

I remember one day when Wanda began thinking maybe one of her ideas was a little too far out. Pausing to stare at me with anxious eyes, she asked, "Jerry, do you think I'm crazy?"

I looked back at her intently and said, "Wanda, sometimes I think all the rest of us are crazy and you're the only sane one."

During one of my visits while she was a patient at Duke Hospital seeking treatment for her cancer, I heard a relative say, "The best descriptive thing you can say about Wanda is simply 'Wanda.'" I wished I had said that. A perfect description of her uniqueness.

Another clue to the way she viewed the world was one of her favorite hobbies—photography. What is the essence of snapping a picture, really? Isn't it capturing a passing moment—a slice of life—forever?

"Time goes too quickly."

The clock keeps on ticking in this world. Fleeting moment follows fleeting moment. So special moments, if we are to fully imprint them in our memory, must be photographed or deeply treasured as they occur. Wanda Sublett did both.

She did so love the special moments of her life: camping with her family, trips to the Eastern Shore, retreats with the youth, assembly programs with the Learning Center (which she helped found).

Wanda's words to the editor of the *Gazette* turned out to be prophetic: "Time goes too quickly."

Her life was ended by cancer much too soon. Wanda fought it valiantly, not wanting to miss the special moments still ahead—graduations and weddings and grandchildren.

All of us desperately wanted it for her—all those special moments. So her death cast a pall of sadness over the entire church family.

In reality, Wanda Sublett did not need a *long* journey to experience a *full* life. And to teach us an important lesson: "A rich life is not measured by how long the moments last, but by how fully we experience each moment along the way."

"Time goes too quickly." So fill each moment to the brim.

In the end, I guess that's the major difference between a journey and a trip. A trip is a necessary instrument by which we reach a destination. A journey is experiencing and celebrating each moment along the way in a manner that molds our lives and the lives of others forever.

But Wanda Sublett actually showed us a third way to travel this earth—treasuring each moment along the way while at the same time keeping our eyes on our eventual destination. Not rushing toward it. Not sacrificing one for the other but finding a balance between the two—the journey and the destination.

On many occasions prior to a youth retreat, I watched Wanda gather her leaders and say, "Nothing is going to happen unless we turn it all over to God." And they would hold hands and pray.

Wanda fought to live because she wanted to be a part of so many things still ahead. But no matter how short or how long our lives last, there are always dreams never quite realized, tasks that we never quite finish, and relationships with still more to explore and experience.

That would be a depressing thought except for the fact that our hope doesn't lie only in this world. Paul says "our citizenship is in heaven" (Phil 3:20a). That's where all our hurts will be made up for and all our unfinished plans are brought to their fullest fruition. Even our bodies will be transformed to "be like his glorious body" (Phil 3:21).

Thank you, Wanda, for reminding us of the urgency of discovering those "Blizzard Blessings" on *this* day.

Yes, "time goes too quickly."

# A Packed Suitcase

It was a familiar invitation: "Percy, would you like to go to…?"

"My suitcase is already packed," Percy would call out before the journey's destination was even announced.

Almost from the beginning, Peggy (Percy) Dye, my wife's aunt, was a woman on the go. Maybe that's why she chose to live in a small cottage that had formerly been a munitions building in the historic village of Harpers Ferry. Percy loved history, but I think it was the river—or "rivers"—that had a lot to do with her choice of homes.

The house was perched near the top of a hill, overlooking the little village of Harpers Ferry and situated approximately 200 yards from Jefferson's Rock. I discovered on one of our visits that Jefferson's Rock is actually three large rocks that received their name after Thomas Jefferson stood on that site and called it "perhaps one of the most stupendous scenes in nature."

As he surveyed the scene from his rock, Jefferson saw the great Shenandoah River joining forces with the mighty Potomac, becoming the Potomac from that point on. In Jefferson's mind, they were combining their power to cut a passage through the Blue Ridge Mountains. Harpers Ferry Gap—sometimes referred to as the "Hole"—is easily seen from Jefferson's Rock.

Symbolically, rivers have represented movement—an almost irresistible journey as the rushing water cuts through clay and rock, reshaping the earth in its refusal to be stopped.

That is also a pretty good description of Percy Dye.

From the beginning she had been a woman on the go, refusing to be stopped. Born in Greene County, North Carolina, on the Edwards farm to Hattie and William Thomas Edwards, Percy was a born adventurer.

Immediately after her graduation from Stantonsburg High School, Percy and a cousin journeyed north to work in one of the New England states in the summer and then traveled south in the winter to work at a hotel in Florida. That was her pattern before finally moving to Washington, DC, to work for a dentist. Percy's brother, Shorty Edwards, my father-in-law, had already established himself in that area.

Having no children, Shorty's offspring—Jean, Pat, Bill, Frances, and Angela—became like Percy's own.

When we drove to Harpers Ferry in September 2002 to conduct Percy's funeral, my wife and I were shown pictures collected by a friend and traveling companion of this dynamic lady.

One picture was of Percy in a complete beekeeper's outfit donned while visiting a bee farm—a symbol of her drive for adventure. Percy did not want to observe life; she wanted to dive in and experience it fully, to become part of what she was seeing.

Another picture showed Percy crammed into a horse-drawn cart with a pile of Amish children. It did not deter her that the cart was being driven by a seven-year-old. And all of this was accomplished with a bum knee, which often made it difficult to walk.

A river is not easily stopped in cutting a passage through whatever lies in its path.

In the years immediately following the purchase of their home, Percy would sit on the porch with her beloved husband, Giff (the dentist she had worked for), and talk to neighbors and townspeople, who were drawn to Percy's magnetic personality.

Even after her husband's sudden, unexpected death, having no immediate family, Percy—like a river—refused to be stopped and still hosted large parties in order to enjoy the company of family and friends..

Although I had already met her when she traveled to our home in Williamsburg, my first visit to her Harpers Ferry cottage was on the occasion of Percy's eightieth birthday—a party that, naturally, she threw for herself.

An intelligent, witty woman, Percy was an avid reader and supporter of the Bolivar/Harpers Ferry Library. Percy especially loved to read about the wives of presidents. No doubt she felt some kinship with these strong women who carried on under demanding circumstances.

In spite of such serious reading material, Percy loved to laugh. Here, again, she refused to go halfway. The laughter would come from deep down, growing in strength until it forced her eyes shut, squeezing happy tears out of the corners of each eye as her entire body shook with the pleasure of it all.

I have been in homes where the television was on constantly, but Percy was the only person I ever knew who kept her TV tuned to the stock market reports day and night. It was interesting to me that she seemed intent on keeping up with the progress of her stock portfolio when, at the same time, she cared little for her accumulating wealth. For Percy, the age of a thing, rather than its elegance or price, determined its value. Antiques made up a big part of her furniture.

While she was generous in giving to many charities and churches, Percy lived very simply, cooking on a tiny gas stove in a miniature kitchen—more suited for a dollhouse than a grownup kitchen. Every night, she would negotiate narrow, winding, metal steps to climb to her sparse bedroom, which was little more than an attic space.

The last time Jean and I visited her—sharing her attic space for sleeping—I heard her go up and down those narrow, winding steps several times during the night. The next morning, I told her I was worried and almost got up to assist her. Percy laughed that big laugh as if it were the most ridiculous thing she had ever heard.

"Just getting some water," she chuckled. Well, of course, a river laughs at silly obstacles.

When I conducted the funeral service for Percy's brother, Shorty, in 1998, she told me that she was surprised Shorty lived so long, because he was always taking risks. I thought, "Adventurous spirits must surely run in this family."

Yes, like a river she was. Always on the go, cutting through whatever needed to be traversed in order to reach her destination.

So it was fitting that Percy died at age eighty-eight the way she lived—not lingering, but still on the way. Still on the go, serving her community, eager for more adventures.

It was also fitting that prior to her death, Percy asked one of her friends to sing "I'll Fly Away" at her funeral. How else could a woman like Percy leave this earth except by taking flight at full speed.

During her funeral, I mentioned that not only do rivers symbolize movement—a journey—but in the scriptures rivers also were understood to be places where God, in all his healing power, was undeniably present. God's people always expected to find God when they gathered at the river.

So it's very understandable that in his great vision of the New Jerusalem—a picture of the resurrected life—John sees a river in the middle of it all.

The suffering people of the world are lined up before the throne of heaven. Then, "the Lamb at the center of the throne will be their shepherd; 'he will lead them to springs of living water.' 'And God will wipe away every tear from their eyes'" (Rev 7:17).

Guiding them to the "springs of the water of life," Jesus breaks the chains and pains of this life and, in a scene of intimate caring, gives us all we need to sustain life forever and ever. And, of course, flowing from the throne was "the river of the water of life" (Rev 22:1).

Just as the great Shenandoah and Potomac joined forces to cut a passage through the Blue Ridge Mountains, the rivers of love and forgiveness have come together to form a mighty river, cutting an opening—a gap—through the mountain of our rebellion and guilt.

And the gap's name is grace.

# Finishing Strong

Looking around the room with a smile, Ken said, "I want us to share some memories. Let's tell some stories about our life together." And they did—some with laughter and some with tears.

Seldom have I seen such a strong finish to a life.

I still own a desk my parents gave me when I left for college. Then, when I got married, they gifted us with a bookshelf. Both are constructed out of dark walnut lumber from trees on what was then my parents' property along Little River in North Carolina.

I treasure them—not only because they were gifts from my parents but also because they have become symbols of a principle I am passionate about: making a good finish.

Somehow, I have always felt that no matter how good a beginning I make, if I do not finish well, I am a failure. I know, logically, that doesn't make sense. Lots of good things can be accomplished along the way even if the finish is weak.

Still, when I began thinking about retirement, my constant prayer was that the church would be on an upswing rather than trending downward. No matter what had happened through the years, I felt my ministry would be tarnished if it did not end strongly. Thankfully, God chose to answer that prayer in the affirmative, as my last year as pastor of Walnut Hills was, statistically at least, one of the most productive in all my time there.

And that desk and bookcase? Well, the man who built them lived a few miles out in the country from my parents' home. He spent his days making all kinds of furniture, working in a simple shop in a remote part of Montgomery County. And yet people would come from big cities all across the state to order pieces of furniture.

They were surprised, but not deterred, when he would tell them in an unhurried drawl, hardly looking up from his workbench, "I might be able to work you in about a year from now." That's about as close as he ever got to catching up with his orders.

The reason for this was quite simple: He would never rush a job, paying close attention to every detail of his craftsmanship. Discerning people know that you can always tell a good workman by the "finish" he puts on a job. Sometimes he was reluctant to let go of a piece of furniture because, as he would say, "It doesn't seem quite finished."

Craftsmen who put a good finish on their work impress me. But it's even more impressive when I see how some put a finish on their life.

Ken Pickin was struggling hard to breathe—aided by an oxygen mask, which was sending a loud rushing current of air into his mouth and nose, making it very difficult for his sporadic words to be understood.

Finally, one afternoon, with friends and family sitting and standing around the room, Ken reached up, pulled the mask—still spilling out a roaring gust of oxygen—away from his face and said, "That's enough. That's enough struggle and pain."

Ken was telling those he loved most that this mask was not the way he wanted to finish his life.

Looking around the room with a smile, he said, "I want us to share some memories. Let's tell some stories about our life together." And they did.

After everyone had a chance to speak, Ken said, his voice growing weaker from the lack of oxygen, but with his arms spread wide to include everyone, "Thank you all for being here."

When his words became difficult to understand, Ken's son, Ben, helped interpret for everyone. "I love you all," Ken said. "Each of you has changed my life." It was a wondrous thing to see someone struggling to draw each breath using his last few breaths to express deep gratitude—delivered with a smile and a thumbs up.

Ken Pickin stands for me as one of the supreme examples of an individual making a strong finish to his earthly journey.

Earlier in the week, as Ken knew his time was growing short, he sent word for me to come to the hospital, even though we had not seen or talked to each other for many years. Some relationships are established quickly and last a lifetime no matter how often it is renewed. Such was ours.

But then a totally unexpected thing happened. Ken asked his wife, Dale, to put a $100 bill in an envelope and give it to me. For some reason, a random thought had led him to believe that he had forgotten to pay me for officiating at their wedding forty-one years earlier.

Dale assured him the best man had taken care of that. It gave us all a chuckle, but it was also another sign that Ken wanted to wrap up all the loose ends in this life before he departed to begin his next life. He did not want to be the victim of a weak finish.

Some of the saddest words in the Bible for me are these: "Do your best to come to me quickly, for Demas, because he loved this world, has deserted me and has gone to Thessalonica" (2 Tim 4:9–10a).

Demas had made a good start. In Paul's letter to Philemon, he makes reference to "Mark, Aristarchus, Demas, and Luke, my fellow workers" (v. 24). Things seem to be getting a little shaky when Paul writes to the Colossians, "Our dear friend Luke, the doctor, and Demas" (Col 4:14). Is a cool wind beginning to blow as Paul refers to Luke as "our dear friend," while Demas is just plain "Demas"?

Then, finally, Paul writes these words to Timothy: "Demas, in love with this present world, has deserted me and gone to Thessalonica." Demas was unable to make a strong finish.

If Ken had his choice, he would still be in his beloved woods hunting deer with his beloved son and special friends. But we seldom have the freedom to choose when our life will end. Thankfully, however, we sometimes have the choice as to how we will react to those things that happen to us—how our life will end.

Following Ken's last breath, I walked into the room with his wife and son for a final prayer of thanksgiving for Ken's life, commending him into the loving hands of our heavenly Father. As we were leaving the room, Ben patted his father's arm, saying quietly, "He was my best friend. He taught me a lot. Now I've got a lot to teach my girls."

As we exited the room, Ben added, "I wish I could be half the man he was." His mother put her arms around him and said, "You already are, Son."

A strong finish had given birth to a strong "beginning again" in countless lives.

Ben paused and took a deep breath before stepping into the hallway to greet a huddle of friends and family.

# Hole in One

"Jerry!" I could hear the excitement in his voice. "I just got a hole in one."

"I know you did, George," I replied. "You showed it to me at Christmas."

George Talley's lovely wife, Jane, to whom he had been married for over fifty years, was deeply supportive of him in all things—including his golf. Knowing that George had been trying for another hole in one since his last one three years prior in 2000, Jane had given George a little box for Christmas.

Clara Jebson

On the outside of the box was a picture of a golfer with the words "Golfer's Dream." When George opened the box, a large black "1" appeared with a hole in its middle.

It was comforting for me to know that there is more than one way to get a hole in one. The golf course method has eluded me thus far.

That was in December. Now it was January, and I was wondering for a moment if George was losing his short-term memory. "Did you forget, George? You already showed me the hole in one Jane gave you for Christmas."

Chuckling, George replied, "No, no, I'm not talking about the Christmas gift. I just made an actual hole in one." The reason I was surprised was that this came on January 2—just eight days after the hole in one gift box.

I had asked George if I could use that story as an illustration in a sermon for the next Sunday. He responded with a wry comment, "Sure, if you tell it right."

"George," I replied, laughing, "are you suggesting I embellish my stories?"

Chuckling, George replied, "However you want to take it, Pastor. However you want to take it."

All of this was floating through my mind on this day as I was working on a New Year's sermon in which I was asking folks to tell me their dreams instead of their resolutions. Resolutions are helpful, I suppose, but they don't seem to last very long. One recent study revealed that only sixty-four percent of resolutions last longer than the first month and only forty-six percent last longer than six months.

On the other hand, I have discovered that dreams are more likely to become guiding forces over a lifetime. Dreams have the power to alter our perception of reality. Dreams enable us to see beyond the obvious to the hidden possibilities of life.

I read or heard somewhere that after the completion of Disney World, someone remarked, "Isn't it too bad that Walt Disney didn't live to see this?" Mike Vance, creative director of Disney Studios, replied, "He did see it. That's why it's here."

Dreams are powerful. Not only do our dreams reveal hidden possibilities, but by voicing our dreams, we also make a commitment to making those dreams come true. But here is where I believe the real power in dreams takes place: learning to listen for God's dreams. I was reflecting on that a few years later while I was preparing the eulogy for Jane. We gathered to celebrate her remarkable life on March 17, 2014.

Jane's unexpected death shocked and deeply saddened all of us who loved this special, warm-hearted woman. But the eulogy came easy, as it always does for a person who is committed to living out God's dreams. "Living out God's dreams," I felt, was the key to understanding the essence of Jane Talley. She was committed to following God's dreams for her life.

While I was working on Jane's service, George reminded me that they had become part of the Walnut Hills family in 2000. "George," I said in surprise, "you've been here much longer than that."

Then I remembered that George and Jane had attended for a while before transferring their church membership. They told me they had made a pledge to the building program at their former church, Covington Baptist in Covington, Virginia. "We have to honor that before we can commit to another church," they had told me.

That was the first time I had heard those words during the many years I had been a pastor. The common practice was that when you leave town and leave a church, all prior commitments are off.

But I shouldn't have been surprised. Covington Baptist Church was my first place of ministry. During the summer following my second year in the seminary, I served as youth director for that good church. I had known Jane and George since 1965 and was aware of their commitment to God's dreams for their lives.

Ryburn T. Stancil was the pastor of Covington. I needed a kind pastor to be patient with a first-time youth minister, and I am forever grateful that he helped build the foundation for my positive view of ministry.

One day while we were reminiscing about those early days, Jane laughed suddenly and said, "Do you remember our nickname for Reverend Stancil?"

"No, I don't think I ever heard that," I replied.

Smiling even more broadly, Jane said, "No Cancel Stancil." We both burst into laughter as Jane explained, "He never met a snowstorm or ice storm big enough to cause him to cancel a service."

Remembering that conversation while working on Jane's celebration service, I thought how that kind of commitment to God and church really defined Jane: She never met a storm big enough to cancel the dreams she felt God had for her life.

"We've got a four-wheel drive, George. Why can't we make it to church?" Or if George was a little tired or not feeling well, he would suggest that they skip Sunday school and just attend worship. Jane's response to that was always the same: "George, we *are* going to Sunday school."

Wherever Jane went, her bright smile spread the good news of God's love and acceptance. During the greeting time in worship, Jane roamed to the far corners of the sanctuary to make sure everyone—especially first-time worshipers—felt welcome.

When her grandchildren came to visit, they laughingly but lovingly told how their grandmother was insistent that they meet everyone. Then they would wait patiently by the car until Jane was certain there was no one left to whom she could offer a word of love and encouragement.

They understood. Jane had heard God's dreams for her life, and she was committed to living them out.

Earlier, during the week of Jane's death, unaware she was even ill, my wife had remarked that following the previous Wednesday night, when Jean's cooking team had prepared the meal, Jane had come up to her with a warm "thank you" and said, "I know how much work goes into preparing a meal for this many people, and I want you to know we never take it for granted."

A simple thing, but an affirmation of Jane's sensitivity to the lifegiving value of heartfelt gratitude.

One of her last acts on this earth was writing a birthday card and a get-well card to church members. After her death, George found the cards lying on her desk awaiting the addresses Jane was too weak to place on the envelopes.

Another dream Jane felt God had given her was a passion for missions and leading others—especially young people—to become involved in missions. That dream took place at a very young age.

At one point in Baptist life, there was a missions organization for young children called "Sunbeams." I have such a clear remembrance of that because of my second-grade teacher, Miss Sally Ewing. A wonderful teacher and devoted member of the First Baptist Church of Mt. Gilead, North Carolina, Miss Ewing periodically held a Sunbeam meeting following school hours in her classroom. My lasting memory of those meetings, regretfully, was not of missions but of the great fear that I was going to miss my bus, the only way I had of getting the two miles to my home.

Jane's biggest memory of Sunbeams, however, was the dream God planted in her heart to lead young people into missions. Following her death, the young girls mission organization at Walnut Hills became known as "Jane's Girls."

Jane's life demonstrated not only the power of dreams but even more the power of listening for God's dreams. That's really the secret to life, isn't it?

I am always deeply moved by the scene in 1 Samuel 3:1–10, where God comes to the young boy Samuel in a dream. Samuel no doubt went to bed expecting to dream his own young boy dreams. At least, it certainly appears he was not expecting to dream God's dreams.

It was not a good time in Israel's history: "In those days the word of the LORD was rare; there were not many visions" (1 Sam 3:1). But during the night there came an unexpected voice: "Samuel." Samuel ran to old Eli, whom he had been assisting, thinking Eli had called him. He never imagined God could be calling since Samuel "did not yet know the LORD" (1 Sam 3:7).

Eli also thought the young boy was dreaming his own dreams and sent him back to bed. It happened a third time, and, finally, in Eli's tired old mind there stirred the possibility that God could once again be speaking. Perhaps a memory of when the word of the Lord was heard often and people saw visions and dreamed God's dreams was revived in Eli's aging heart.

Finally, Eli told Samuel, "'Go and lie down, and if he calls you, say, "Speak, Lord, for your servant is listening."'" So Samuel went and lay down in his place" (1 Sam 3:9).

And it happened just that way. God said to Samuel, "'See, I am about to do something in Israel that will make the ears of everyone who hears about it tingle'" (1 Sam 3:11).

Jane Talley knew about both ears tingling with the excitement of hearing God's dreams.

George would sometimes tell Jane that he felt like she was an angel sent down to show the rest of us how to live. He was probably on to something. What is an angel except one who refuses to be stuck with earthbound dreams, limited dreams? An angel knows about heavenly dreams and the possibility of hearing God's dreams even in another time—this time—when once again the world feels void of an authentic word from God.

So, George, I'm happy you made another hole in one. As the front of that Christmas gift box said, it's a "Golfer's Dream." But I know you'll understand if I tell you that Jane's dreams impress me far more than a golfer's. Jane heard God's dream for her life and lived it to the fullest.

No embellishment is needed for that story to leave me breathless as I seek to hear a voice and catch a vision along my own journey toward Mullinix, that place of authentic discipleship.

# Teaching Promotion?

"Congratulations," I said to Gail Jenner. We were talking casually during the coffee connection in the hospitality center following the morning worship service at Walnut Hills Baptist Church.

I had just asked Gail, a gifted teacher, what she was teaching and when her class of ladies was meeting. "Oh," she replied quickly, "I'm not teaching women anymore. I'm working with children now."

I offered my congratulations and added, "You have been promoted."

Gail was taken aback by my response but quickly recovered as she replied, "I like that. Can I use it?"

"Of course," I laughed as I turned to grab another slice of cheese to place between a couple whole wheat crackers.

Later, on the way home, our brief conversation stirred some memories of a distant past. My Uncle Rankin, Daddy's older brother, was the Sunday school superintendent in our little frame country church, Calvary Baptist, approximately halfway between Mt. Gilead and Wadeville, North Carolina.

Sunday activities could not begin until Uncle Rankin stepped into the center of the empty area between the big potbelly stove and the pulpit, cleared his throat importantly, and intoned in a solemn voice, "Our golden text for this morning is…"

Uncle Rankin would then read the passage of Scripture that the Baptist Sunday School Board in Nashville had selected for emphasis on that day. After offering some brief comments on the scripture, followed by an announcement or two, Uncle Rankin would announce, "You may now go to your classes."

For as long as I could remember, that's how our Sundays at Calvary Baptist Church had begun. We knew of no other way. I was convinced as a young boy that there was something magical about Uncle Rankin's words—so magical that Sunday school and "preaching" would not happen if Sunday morning began any other way.

So I will never forget the year my church world was turned upside down. Someone on the nominating committee, no doubt in an uncharacteristically reckless mood, suggested that Uncle Rankin be moved from his assumed lifetime role as Sunday school superintendent to teacher of the junior boys. The immediate reaction throughout the countryside was no less shocking and earth-rattling than impeaching a sitting president. Uncle Rankin was dumbfounded—wondering what he had done or who had it in for him.

The poor chairman of the nominating committee pleaded for him to "just try it for a while." If Uncle Rankin was surprised and his ego hurt over what all of us at the time saw as a *demotion*, I was even more shocked and disappointed. My church world was shaken to its core. Calvary Baptist Church would never be the same. I had no idea how our Sundays would even begin.

I was secretly hoping Uncle Rankin would give the nominating committee an emphatic "No!" That he was called by God Almighty to stand and pronounce, much like Moses when he offered the Ten Commandments to the children of Israel—"Our golden text for this morning is…"

But after much soul-searching and talking it over with his family, my uncle decided to give it a try.

I can't even remember how our Sundays began from that time on—I was walking around in a thick, confused fog. Somehow, we must have muddled through because the church didn't close its doors. In fact, they are still open to this day, although the little red-shingled frame building was long ago replaced by a sturdy brick structure.

I do, however, have a vivid memory of the nominating committee coming to Uncle Rankin two years later and asking him to serve as Sunday school superintendent once again. I was terribly disappointed, but at the same time had great admiration for him, when Uncle Rankin declined their offer with the explanation, "I just can't leave my junior boys." This time, the nominating committee was as shocked as Uncle Rankin had been two years earlier.

It took me many years to understand what Uncle Rankin meant. He had made the joyous discovery that moving from "golden text" status to teaching some rowdy junior boys was a *promotion* instead of a *demotion*. What higher calling can there be than to have a part in shaping young lives and helping young minds discover the truths of Christianity—truths that would guide them the rest of their lives.

Change is hard—for those initiating the change and those caught up in it. Our first reaction to change is often a sense of loss, of grief. Change means we have lost something. As a young boy, I was certain we had lost the ability to be church with my uncle no longer pronouncing the golden text. But Uncle Rankin refused to let change keep him from making a difference. In fact, change brought him a new beginning and a richer experience. Church was better than ever for him as he talked about those junior boys with a happy glint in his eyes.

God's call usually involves change. Jesus could not have made it any clearer when he said, "'Truly I tell you, unless you change and become like little children, you will never enter the kingdom of heaven'" (Matt 18:3). As hard as we may fight it, change is taking place around us all the time. Our response to it determines whether that change makes life better or worse for ourselves and others.

So congratulations, Gail—and Uncle Rankin. You have embraced change and taken a giant step toward Mullinix, that metaphorical place of mature discipleship.

Any way you look at it, that's a breathtaking promotion.

*Still Going to Mullinix*

# Part Four

A Breathtaking Journey

Is Sometimes Suspenseful

# Fishing Suspects

David's face was beginning to turn the ashen shade of his thick gray hair as he turned to me and asked anxiously, "Jerry, do you think they're shooting at us?"

"Couldn't be," I replied with more confidence than I was feeling. "They can see we're just fishing."

A longtime member of our church and First Colony neighbor, David Fletcher, had been promising for years that he would take me fishing on the James River. On a mild spring Monday morning, David called and asked if this was a good time.

I tried to take most Monday mornings off for some restorative recreation, so this invitation seemed a perfect fit. Many of my colleagues chose Friday as their day of rest. As I heard one of them say, "I'm so discouraged on Mondays that I refuse to waste my one day off when I feel so low."

But with my personality, once I began the week, my mind could not relax until the Sunday worship services were complete. I immediately accepted David's invitation on this lovely Monday morning. David had a quiet manner that made him easy to be with. A few hours of restful fishing on the James was just what the doctor ordered.

My anticipation was high as we met at the First Colony marina, just a half mile from my front door. It's an easy walk, which my youngest grandson, Brent, and I—along with one or two granddogs (however many happen to be visiting)—make every week or so on our way to romp or fish on the beach.

"I'll bring the bait and a couple sandwiches," David said. "Just bring your rod and reel and a thermos of water for yourself."

"Think I can handle that," I said cheerfully, hanging up the phone.

The day was full of promise as David and I climbed into his seventeen-foot aluminum boat, which had seen its best years but was still able to serve our needs quite well. I took a seat near the bow since David was in the stern maneuvering the small motor.

As he skillfully steered the boat toward the middle of the James, David said with an optimistic smile, "There's a creek not far upriver where I usually have a lot of luck."

It was a lovely, quiet spot—just what I had been looking for. It was an extra bonus that we actually hauled in a few medium-sized fish.

I was quite satisfied, but David wanted something bigger. Moving quietly out of the pastoral creek, David suddenly gunned the motor to its highest capacity (which wasn't very high) as we sped down the middle of the river, bouncing along on the small but choppy waves. "There's a hole down here where I've caught some bigger fish," David hollered over the roar of the straining motor.

After a couple miles of racing through the water, David killed the engine and threw a small anchor overboard. "Let's try this for a while," he said.

Before casting my line into the brackish water—the James is a mixture of fresh and salt water before it turns completely salty farther down—I looked around at our surroundings. Spotting several buildings on the western bank of the river, I asked, "Is that the Surry Nuclear Plant?"

"Yep," David replied. "I try not to get too close since 9/11."

We seemed to be fairly close, but I trusted David's experience to know the definition of "too close." In the next few minutes, I wondered if my trust was seriously misplaced.

First of all, I watched a helicopter take flight and head in a direct line toward us. Thinking they would probably just fly on over, I began casting over the side of the boat. I quickly lost interest in the bobbing cork as I noticed that the helicopter was lingering directly above our heads. I watched as an occupant opened the side door to get a better look at us—his feet dangling over the edge of the helicopter's open door.

When the man took out binoculars, I gave him an uneasy smile and a tentative wave. "Just a Baptist layman and his pastor on an innocent Monday morning fishing excursion," I yelled up at him, not really believing he could hear.

Suddenly I realized that maybe I shouldn't have revealed our denomination—what with suspicions being like they were. The man with the binoculars may have been Episcopalian.

"They'll just take a good look and move on," David said, but his voice betrayed his own growing anxiety. Just then our stress leaped to an infinitely higher level as we heard a series of gunshots above the noise of the chopper.

"Surely they're not shooting at us!" David exclaimed.

"They're shooting at something," I yelled back over the cacophony of noise. Instinctively, I ducked as low as I could in the small boat, which wasn't nearly as low as I would have liked to have been.

Fortunately, we had heard no whine of bullets splitting the air above our heads, nor had we received any instructions from the helicopter to vacate the area. But, as I said, this was only a few short months following the terrorist attack on the twin towers, and everyone's nerves were on edge.

Actually, *our* nerves were just about to fall *over* the edge, as David lost his struggle to sound casual while muttering, "Maybe we better find another spot."

We did.

A few days later, a friend who has worked at the Surry Nuclear Plant for many years found my account of that day much more amusing than I did. "Following 9/11 we do check out people who come around—even Baptist preachers."

For some reason he thought that was hilarious and burst into a spasm of laughter. Finally regaining his composure, he continued, "But they would probably have left you alone after a few minutes—especially if you had actually caught one of those largemouth basses you're always bragging about." This brought on another irritating spasm of laughter.

I did not feel bad about interrupting him. "What about all that shooting?" I persisted.

He was thoughtful for a minute before answering: "I'm not sure, but there's a firing range near that spot. Someone was probably getting in a little target practice." I didn't respond to his amusement, so he added, "Pastor, we don't shoot at random fishermen—even if they aren't catching anything."

I thanked him for nothing and told him he sounded much more amused than reassuring. That brought on another fit of laughter, which followed me as I hurried down the church hallway.

During my years of ministry, some Mondays have been more restful than others. I don't need to tell you where this one fell on the scale of quiet, restorative days. This event did, however, underline for me the extent of our society's suspicions of each other.

The other day I watched with interest as the director of a documentary on Mister Rogers of the famed *Mister Rogers' Neighborhood* explained his project. Seems he started getting social media messages from all over. The crux of most of them was, "Please don't destroy my childhood."

Suspicious of kindness and goodness, the correspondents were fearful what they saw of Mister Rogers on television may not have been real.

As it turns out, such fears were totally unfounded as the director of the documentary assured them his research revealed that Mister Rogers was an even *better* person in real life than on television.

"He had a certain swagger about him," the producer said, "a swagger that came from his belief that he could change the world—change the world with love, which, as he kept saying, was the root of all good things in the world."

No doubt we live in a dangerous, uncertain world. But if we are not careful, that fact can make us suspicious and fearful of most things and most people—leaving no room for trust and love. We can easily lose our "swagger" in believing in the power of love, kindness, and goodness.

But maybe Jesus was giving us a solution to that dilemma—or at least a hint of a solution—in Matthew: "'I am sending you out like sheep among wolves. Therefore be as shrewd as snakes and as innocent as doves'" (Matt 10:16).

Do you think maybe Jesus is suggesting that we can be wary of people and situations without becoming full-blown cynics? Is it possible to risk being vulnerable to the actions of another while at the same time maintaining an innocence of spirit—holding on to the goal of Christlike love and trust?

Now that's a breathtaking thought.

*Still Going to Mullinix*

By the way, it's time for another fishing trip on the James. When David calls, I will have no hesitation about going. I refuse to allow the distrustful—even dangerous—actions of others keep me from "showing up" in those places where my intentions are both innocent and good.

Risk is a constant in this world, but both fishing on the James and being part of the difficult work of establishing the kingdom of God "on earth as it is in heaven" are certainly worth the risk.

I guess wisdom does demand, however, that I keep a reasonable distance from the Surry Nuclear Power Plants of this world.

After all, a certain snakelike shrewdness is required even as I seek to be as "innocent as a dove" along the journey to Mullinix.

# Violence in the Home

The call jolted me from my comfortable electric La-Z-Boy chair where thirty minutes earlier I had settled in for the evening.

"Pastor, you need to come over as quickly as you can!"

"What's wrong?"

The panicked voice answered with a slight tremor, "My wife just shot at me."

I was accustomed, as a pastor, to being called out at all times of the day and night, but most of those calls did not involve firearms. Unfortunately, a few did, as emotions can accelerate quickly and dangerously in domestic altercations—especially when there are broken promises and deep hurts, sometimes fueled by alcohol.

I knew there had been high tension in this home because Cliff (not his real name, of course) had become involved with a woman at work. That, too, happened far more than I like to remember.

"I assume you weren't hit," I replied.

"No. She hit the bookcase. I know you can calm her down." Cliff hesitated before adding more quietly, "I don't want to get the police involved."

I knew both Cliff and his wife, Dorothy (also fictional name), well. They had been strong leaders in the church for many years. Cliff, like many we were fortunate to have over the years, was regarded as a gifted teacher with a devoted following, and Dorothy held a variety of leadership positions.

With our personal history I was pretty confident I could defuse the situation without the convoluted complications of outside involvement. I threw on a jacket and headed toward their home, praying all the way for calm for them and wisdom for myself.

When I walked up to the front door, Cliff opened it before I had time to ring the doorbell. I immediately noticed two large suitcases just inside the door. My eyes lingered on them for a second as I realized the cause of the explosion.

Cliff's eyes were wide with alarm and guilt as he burst out, "Pastor, I know what you're going to say, and I agree with you. What I am doing is wrong." His chin was set stubbornly as he continued, "But I'm going to do it anyway."

His emphatic words didn't leave much room for a response, so I walked past him into the den, where I found Dorothy sitting with her hands in her lap. The revolver lay on an end table beside her. She looked as if she were almost in a trance as her glazed eyes lifted slowly to look at me.

"Jerry, you know I didn't intend to hit him," she mumbled with a catch in her voice. "I'm a very good shot. I hit what I aim at."

"I know, honey," I said soothingly as I knelt before her. I held her hand for a few moments before adding, "Cliff didn't leave me much to say. He said he knew what he was doing was wrong, but he was going to do it anyway."

She nodded slightly and said slowly, "That's what he told me. That's why I shot into the bookcase. Just to get his attention and let him know how much he was hurting me." She began crying quietly, and I leaned over to hug her. "He doesn't care. I guess there's nothing left to say or do," she whispered into my shoulder as she continued to sob softly.

Cliff's hesitant voice came from the front foyer, "Well, I'm going."

Dorothy refused to look at him as I called out, "Stay in touch." This was in the days before cellphones, so I had no way of reaching him unless he called me.

"I'll give you a call," Cliff said over his shoulder as the door closed behind him.

Following the clanging of the heavy front door, there was an eerie silence. In an instant the house had become as quiet and empty as any home I have ever known.

I pulled up a chair, and Dorothy and I talked for about two hours before I was satisfied that it was safe to leave her alone. As I stood to leave, however, I looked down at the revolver and said, "Do you think it might be wise for me to take your gun with me?"

She paused a moment as she looked into my eyes and then nodded slowly. "Probably a good idea," she said.

Many years prior to her death, I stumbled across that revolver, which I had hidden on the top shelf in my closet when I returned home that night. I had forgotten all about it. On my next visit with Dorothy in her new house, where she was doing a good job of putting her life back together, I told her I had found the gun on a top shelf under a stack of sweaters.

"Would you like it back?" Not only did she live alone, but I knew she had always enjoyed target practice. That's one reason I knew she had never meant to shoot her husband. She was too good of a marksman to miss at that range.

Smiling wryly, she replied, "I have no use for it. I haven't touched a revolver since that night. Get rid of it." It was obvious the gun brought back too many bitter memories—memories that had also flooded my mind when I had unexpectedly come across it.

Cliff's death came several years before Dorothy's. But I had occasion to meet him at a gathering a couple years after that fateful night and asked how he was doing. "I'm still teaching," he said, smiling.

I looked at him quizzically, studying his face. "I know what you're thinking," he said as his smile faded. "And, yes, there are parts of the Bible I have to leave out in my teaching."

"That's the sad part of trying to live with the Bible as our guide, isn't it?" I replied. Cliff stared at me quietly but expectantly. "The parts we have to leave out. The parts that are too hard to accept—or follow."

Cliff bowed his head and whispered, barely loud enough for me to hear, "Yes, Pastor. I guess you're right."

The apostle Paul seemed to have something of the same trouble. He, like Cliff, said he knew the right thing to do but at times could not do it. Or maybe Paul, too, simply refused to do it: "I do not understand what I do. For what I want to do I do not do, but what I hate I do" (Rom 7:15).

Now all that can get pretty discouraging. But over in his first letter to Timothy, Paul also talks about fighting "the good fight of the faith" (6:12).

Here, it seems to me—and to several commentators I consulted—that Paul is not talking about overcoming outside competition, as he does in other places. Rather, he is more interested in the possibility of winning the harder fight of overcoming the worst in himself.

That's a tough battle, but Paul seems to believe it can be won through faith in Christ, "who gives life to everything" (1 Tim 6:13). It's comforting to know that Paul, who struggled like us in dealing with those inner conflicts between good and evil, believed the battle could be won.

I needed to hear that. The journey to Mullinix might never be completed if I must hold my breath and detour around every difficult place of discipleship.

# Preparing for the Worst

It was a test, he said. A test to challenge himself. How long would he be able the evade law enforcement officers in the mountainous region of western North Carolina?

To get the game started, the newspaper reported that James Andrew Finley Jr. had shot and slashed to death two twenty-four-year-old campers in the Linville Gorge area.

Based on the latest information of sightings, Finley had moved eastward into the Piedmont region of North Carolina. Upon arriving for a family visit, I discovered that a manhunt command center was set up in the little community of Pekin, just five miles down the road from my parents' home. Evidence showed that Finley had abandoned a stolen car after a high-speed chase in that community.

He was getting closer. I have tried never to anticipate the worst, but I have always exercised a certain caution in the face of potential danger. My wife simply says I worry too much. Maybe. But then I point out Jesus's words in Luke: "'But understand this: If the owner of the house had known at what hour the thief was coming, he would not have let his house be broken into'" (12:39).

Sometimes caution is required. My parents and I began preparations.

State and local police officers wearing bulletproof vests walked from house to house telling the residents to stay inside, lock all the doors, and not go to work that day.

Low-flying helicopters flew directly over my parents' home for the next two days as groups of men with tracking dogs, along with police cars, formed a diligent parade along N.C. 703, running next to my parents' front yard. Television news programs interviewed mild-mannered men holding shotguns and rifles, saying, "Normally, I would never lift a gun to anyone, but if he threatens my family, I want to be ready."

My two sisters and brother came over the first night of my visit, hoping my parents would go home with them. After they resisted, my siblings finally conceded, "Jerry, since you're here, we won't insist Mother and Daddy go kicking and screaming."

I have learned to appreciate even half-hearted votes of confidence in a highly skeptical world. But now I felt a tremendous responsibility for the safety of my parents, who were both in failing health. For one thing, they could no longer hear very well—meaning I had to do the hearing for three people.

"Guess we better make all the preparations we can," I said on the way to replacing all the burned-out outside light bulbs. Next, I dug out my father's automatic .22 rifle, which felt strange since I had only held rifles and shotguns in preparation for hunting forays many years earlier during my high school days.

I wasn't surprised that it took Daddy quite a while to locate ammunition for the rifle since he hadn't used it for a while either. Before I climbed into bed later that evening, I placed the rifle on the floor within easy reach and the cartridges on the nightstand.

Unlike Barney, the deputy sheriff of Mayberry fame, I laid out more than one bullet. It was an eerie, unnatural feeling—this preparing for the worst.

Unfortunately, I have known a lot of folks who have adopted that posture as a lifestyle—always expecting the worst, always looking around the next corner for the "crisis of the day." Too often, that approach became a self-fulfilling prophecy. Such folks always seemed to find more crises than the ordinary population. Did their actions promote, and even create, the worst?

Most days—oh, I've had my share, I suppose—I do not live waiting for the other shoe to drop or the next tragedy to rear its ugly head. I do confess that at one point in my ministry—when our church had experienced a series of tragedies, one following fast on the other—I jumped involuntarily and cringed every time the phone rang, especially after bedtime.

Expecting the worst is unnatural for me, even as I recognized the necessity of such preparations at this time. It felt particularly odd when I turned off the fan, which had droned our family to sleep, shutting out all outside noises, ever since our children were infants.

During this night, however, I *wanted* to hear all outside noises. I lay alertly listening to the night sounds of the country for the first time in a long time—the crickets and tree frogs and whippoorwills—wondering at how something so pleasant could contain such potential danger.

I wondered even more if I would sleep at all that night.

That's when a face from the past appeared unexpectedly in my restless mind. The face belonged to Dr. Brown, my New Testament professor in seminary. The unique thing about this professor was that he insisted on our memorizing passages of Scripture. Not only did he insist; he tested us on them. It was impossible to pass his class without a vast store of memorized Scripture.

We all protested long and hard. "We can look them up. Why waste so much time memorizing all those passages?" Our complaining fell on deaf ears.

In the years following, I learned to appreciate Dr. Brown more and more. In times of crisis when I needed to offer words of comfort, I did not have to search for them. They were readily available, still resting in parts of my brain.

Now, as I lay quietly, intently alert at even the tiniest creak of that old house, built in the mid-1940s, a few of those memorized verses began a silent parade through my mind:

Come to me, all you who are weary and burdened, and I will give you rest. (Matt 11:28)

Peace I leave with you; my peace I give you.... Do not let your hearts be troubled and do not be afraid. (John 14:27)

Rejoice in the Lord always. I will say it again: Rejoice!... And the peace of God, which transcends all understanding, will guard your hearts and your minds in Christ Jesus. (Phil 4:4, 7)

"I see what you mean, Dr. Brown," I muttered quietly. Somewhere well past midnight, I felt my eyes closing as I whispered a "thank you" to that old professor. But mostly I offered a deep "thank you" to God that even if the worst came, I was still, as Paul wrote to those Philippian Christians, "in Christ Jesus."

When sleep finally came, I did not awaken until the sun rose, filling my bedroom with its brilliant morning light.

Note: In less than two days of searching in the woods of Montgomery County, Finley was arrested for the Linville Gorge murders in a hunting lodge approximately ten miles from my parents' home.

# Fear of the Unknown

"Mother, what could that be?" I could not keep the tremor out of my little boy's voice.

A spine-tingling howl shattering the normally pastoral peace of our home seemed to grow louder and more unearthly each day as the sun began to set behind the large oak trees clustered behind our small frame house. Today, a young boy would no doubt attribute the cry to some fearful zombie alien. But I was unacquainted with such things as a five-year-old in the mid-1940s.

I've always found it a little strange that some of my most vivid memories occurred when I was a preschooler. People who have trouble remembering any of their childhood have disputed that claim. But prior to my mother's death in 2007, she would confirm the accuracy of almost all of my early childhood memories. She did feel that I embellished a few of them, but her mother's love was willing to extend a certain latitude.

One of my early memories is of chasing my brother, almost two years younger, up busy Highway 109 with our mother struggling to keep up—frantically urging me on. We were both terribly fearful that a speeding car would run him over if he veered even slightly from the shoulder of the road.

Kent was determined to find our father, who was in the sawmill business at the time and often worked in remote forests. This initial toddler confidence in reaching his destination probably contained the seeds for my brother's later decision to enter the Peace Corps and journey to far places.

I was more drawn to the security of home—which is an interesting note on how unexpected turns can alter our imagined paths. I ended up being the only one of four children to live in another state since my mid-twenties, while Kent and my two sisters, Ginny and Donna, settled close to our childhood home.

When I would finally catch up to the adventurous three-year-old, with Mother calling out for me to hold him until she caught up, Kent would begin biting my hands and arms or any piece of exposed flesh. Switching hands rapidly, I was somehow able to hang on until Mother arrived.

But back to my thoughts on memory. I've also discovered that fear is always a great aid to memory. In addition, my most clearly defined "fear memories" are those that fall into the category of the unknown and unidentifiable.

That's where that otherworldly moan I mentioned earlier comes in. No one could identify its origin, but my active childish imagination conjured up all kinds of grotesque creatures who could easily overpower my small frame and hungrily tear into my tender flesh with far greater consequences than my brother's needle-like bites.

At the time, my great-uncle, John McNeil—the confirmed bachelor brother of my paternal grandmother—lived in a little cabin down a lane leading from the rear of our home, across a small creek and set in the middle of a small clearing surrounded by thick woods. The cabin had neither electricity nor indoor plumbing and was totally encased in shadows when the sun began setting. I could not imagine spending the night there.

One day at twilight, John came knocking on our back-porch screen door and asked in an unusually grave tone—in stark contrast to his usual jocular mood—if he could speak to my father. I stayed just close enough to hear their whispered conversation.

"Johnie, don't know if ya heared it, but the howling seems to be gittin' louder." I could tell he was shaken. Well, no wonder. He lived in a scary house surrounded by dark, scary woods. Now he had to try to sleep surrounded by a scary, mysterious howl.

"Yeah, I've noticed," my father replied softly, trying to keep me from hearing and increasing my anxiety. It didn't work. Their overheard conversation only served to enhance my nightmares later that night with images of monsters too frightening to speak of.

My father's parting words of assurance were, "We'll get some folks together and see what we can find out tomorrow night." Uncle John nodded slowly as he reluctantly turned to walk the dark path, across the little wooden bridge, back to his lonely, shadowy cabin.

The thought crossed my mind that we should invite him to camp out on the back porch since we didn't have any more beds. But I did not have the confidence to be that assertive at that young age.

I surely didn't want anything to happen to Uncle John. Since he had no steady job—only occasional odd ones—he was our only grownup playmate.

Well, that isn't completely accurate. Our next-door neighbor—another Mrs. Haywood—would get down on her hands and knees on her front porch with my older sister, Ginny, along with my younger brother and me. The porch was full of ants darting here and there and occasionally disappearing into the cracks between the narrow boards.

"You see that little one," she would say softly. "His father probably got stepped on, and he's taking that tiny bread crumb to help his mother feed the rest of the family." In her imagination, all the ants had mothers and fathers and siblings, and their continued existence was crucial for the rest of the family.

As a result, she taught us to be very careful not to step on any of the ants—seeing them as fellow travelers with human emotions and characteristics and responsibilities.

I attribute much of my deep feeling for the sacredness of all life to that sweet lady's big heart and magnanimous imagination.

Maybe I'm sharing too much when I confess that I still go out of my way to avoid stepping on ants and other insects on our large front porch in First Colony near Jamestown, Virginia. Surprising twinges of guilt also inflict me when my wife complains of ants in the kitchen and I dutifully put out the obligatory poison.

That's when I see Mrs. Haywood on her hands and knees, her kind eyes following the paths of the scurrying ants. Silly questions pop into my grownup mind: "How many ant families am I destroying with this sticky dab of death? Which son or daughter isn't going to return home to eat with the rest of the family tonight?"

As embarrassing as it is to admit that, it serves to affirm the power of early impressions painted on the mostly blank canvas of young minds.

But our other adult playmate, Uncle John, would keep us laughing with his funny, wrinkled faces. We enjoyed his company so much that we even dared to venture back to his isolated cabin from time to time. Of course, that was only when the sun was shining brightly.

In all these many years later, I have failed to find a wink as classic and endearing as Uncle John's. His exaggerated wink screwed up the entire left side of his deeply lined face and invited us into a secret world that belonged only to the three of us.

Uncle John also taught us that green snakes were harmless—which turned out to be dangerous knowledge for Kent and me. Late one afternoon, we climbed after one of those harmless ("Uncle John *said*") critters so far up a big oak tree in the backyard that mother almost called the Mt. Gilead volunteer fire department to get us down.

We never caught the green snake and finally made our precarious trip down the tree with Mother standing underneath, her arms outstretched to break our fall.

I wasn't aware of it at the time, but Uncle John also taught us that the deep pleasures of life come through simple things and that one can find peace and joy with a minimum of material things and a total absence of wide-ranging travels. Or even travels beyond the borders of Montgomery County.

Uncle John never drove and never owned a car. Walking placed within his reach all the interesting and pleasurable things he needed or wanted. In his middle years Uncle John would seek out the company of a woman, Retta (short for Henrietta) Haywood, who, like Uncle John, never married. Here again, the simple company of Retta seemed to be enough.

One day during my early teen years, I caught them on a front porch swing of the residence where Retta was working as a housekeeper at the time. I kept coming around to watch because this was something completely foreign to my previous experiences with Uncle John.

The remarkable thing was that during those three hours or so that I watched them—trying, but obviously failing, to be discreet—I never saw them speak or even touch hands. Of course, when Uncle John caught my eye as I peeped around a corner, he gave me that big wink, rivaled only by Popeye's.

Popeye entered my life when I was twelve and black-and-white television finally arrived in Mt. Gilead. But Popeye had the unfair prop of a big pipe, so I still considered Uncle John the champion winker. He needed no props.

On that day, unknown to both of us, he was also sharing the secret of courting. "Nothin' to it, Son. Ya don' need to talk 'r touch 'r ev'n swing. Ya jist set and *be*." That was a comforting lesson for a shy teenager who had trouble finding the right words— or any words, for that matter—in the presence of the opposite sex.

Years later, while helping people through many difficult, thorny relationships as a pastor, the picture of Uncle John and Retta smiling in satisfied silence on that porch swing flashes into my mind. I wish we could all find the secret of such simple togetherness—just "settin' and bein'." Why do we make it so complicated?

One of the more useful things I learned from Uncle John was that when he would noisily expel gas—his diet seemed to afford him an abundance of gas—he would jerk his head around quickly and exclaim, "Stepped on 'nother frog, boys," and wink that big Popeye wink. Kent and I were terribly frustrated that we could never find those squashed frogs—especially since there were so many of them.

Not everyone is as pleased as I am when I pass on that little piece of family legacy to the younger members of our clan. But I am compelled to do so in loving memory of my first adult playmate.

True to my daddy's promise, late the next afternoon, a small group of men gathered quietly in our backyard. My father, Uncle Branson, and our next-door neighbor all carried loaded 12-gauge shotguns. That didn't calm my anxiety at all.

Uncle John was there but declined to go since, as he explained, he possessed no gun. As I looked into his ashen face, I sensed relief rather than deprivation over the lack of a firearm. But it was Uncle John, so I gave him the benefit of the doubt.

As I watched the silent group of men shuffle off into the woods toward the eerie howling, which, strangely, seemed to be a little weaker than usual on this evening, a paralyzing fear gripped me. I wondered if I would ever see my father—or any of them—again. The loaded shotguns they carried would have little effect if the creature was as big and powerful as I imagined.

Long, agonizing hours passed as I waited anxiously on the screened back porch. In reality, my mother said only an hour and a half had passed before the small group exited the woods and reassembled in our backyard with the news. They were all much more relaxed as they held their now unloaded guns casually and revealed the source of our fears.

Mr. H. A. Nanney, a legendary Mt. Gilead school principal, was also a legendary hunter, and one of his coonhounds had run head-on into a tree during an especially dark night. The blue tick hound was so injured that he could only lie at the base of the tree and howl imploringly.

My father notified Mr. Nanney, who went immediately to retrieve his beloved dog, and our quiet country evenings were once again filled with an extraordinary simplicity and peace, with only the chirping of tree frogs and the lonely call of whippoorwills from across the creek next to Uncle John's cabin. Even the blue tick hound recovered after being placed in a week or two of concussion protocol.

I was greatly relieved, although secretly disappointed, that the answer to one of my greatest fears at that time was as simple as an injured dog. Before the arrival of television, we had to create our own entertainment, and if nothing else, this had certainly been entertaining.

From time to time I remember that long-ago episode—especially when fear intrudes into my life. I'm sure that early fear was so great because its origin was unknown.

That also seems to be the pattern of many of my later fears—the unknown brings the deepest fear. Some of the most agonizing days I have spent with my parishioners have been those in which we were awaiting results of tests for suspected but as yet unidentified illnesses.

It has also been my experience that many of those fears—maybe most—were of no more consequence than an injured canine.

All of that makes me appreciate even more Paul's reminder to the Corinthians: "Therefore we are always confident and know that as long as we are at home in the body we are away from the Lord. For we live by faith, not by sight" (2 Cor 5:6–7).

We cannot know what our future holds. God knows we have enough trouble understanding what's right in front of us. But since we "walk by faith," we no longer need to hold our breath, wondering what mystery awaits us around the next bend.

# Fear of the Unseen

Pa-Pa dropped me off in front of his country store, telling me to go into his house across the dirt road from the store and settle in. Of course, it didn't take long for an eight-year-old to settle his belongings, spending only one night with Pa-Pa and his adult daughter, my Aunt Alta, in the little community of Chip.

I usually rode with Pa-Pa wherever he went in his green Ford pickup—as I have recounted in other stories. But on this occasion, he had promised to give a ride to a man living alone with no way to get to his doctor.

Pickups today hold an entire family of five comfortably—plus Max, their Doberman Pinscher. This was in 1948, however, and my Pa-Pa's pickup, with the gear shift angling over the middle of the front seat, was just big enough for two people.

In addition, social distancing was being practiced in the 1940s and early 1950s as a result of the fear of polio. So besides a lack of room in his pickup, Pa-Pa was reluctant to have me sit in close proximity to his sick neighbor.

That's why I now found myself standing alone in front of a red-shingled shed. The shed was located about thirty yards across the store yard and to the left of its front steps.

That shed has a special memory for me.

When I was four or five years old, I followed Mother and her sisters down the rows of my Pa-Pa's cotton field, dragging a heavy burlap sack. I tried to pick cotton, but my small fingers were not skillful enough to avoid the sharp points of the cotton boll. Little dots of blood were enough to send me racing to Mother for comfort. As she straightened her aching back from bending over the cotton rows, I realized I had at least one advantage—I was so short that I did not have to bend over in my poor attempt to pick from the cotton plants.

My disadvantage, however, was lacking the strength to drag the heavy sack to the end of each row, even without a load of cotton.

I did, however, manage to pluck a few balls of the white fluffy lint from their threatening lair. So just before my limited energy was totally exhausted, I dragged the sack down the hill to the red-shingled shelter where Pa-Pa stood ready to weigh the cotton and then pay the workers according to the amount of cotton they had picked.

As I proudly handed my sack to Pa-Pa, he placed it on the scales and made a big show of reading the gauge. "Ah, law," he said, smiling down at me. "You had you a right big day, Son."

*Day* was an exaggeration since it was not yet noon, but Pa-Pa knew I was probably finished for the day. He then reached into his pocket, rattled a few coins, and made a big show of handing me fifteen cents—two nickels and five pennies. "Yeah, Son, you done right good for yourself," he said with a chuckle rattling deep in his throat. "Now don't you spend it all in one place." His big signature laugh followed me all the way up the slight incline to the store.

That was the first money I ever earned for "real labor." I looked at each coin proudly before placing it carefully in the right front pocket of my cottonfield-soiled jeans. When my Pa-Pa had told me not to spend it all in one place, he knew I would immediately run into his country store and buy an orange Truade drink and several pieces of two-for-a-penny candy. That soda was the most refreshing, and the candy was the sweetest I had ever had. I was experiencing the unfamiliar satisfaction of buying something with money I had "earned."

Now, three years later, I was standing in front of that shelter, idly throwing rocks toward the empty pasture just to the left of the dusty two-lane road.

At that time in my life, most of my idle time was spent either tossing small rocks into the air and hitting them with a strip of wood I had smoothed for a handle at one end—or, if I had no stick bat, seeing how far I could throw the rocks. Often, I would do this until the sun set and it became too dark to see the tossed pebbles.

I have always maintained that particular childhood exercise helped develop my eye-hand coordination as I later played baseball for the Mt. Gilead Lion's Club Little League team and later for Mt. Gilead High School and the Albemarle entry into the American Legion league.

But on this day in 1948, as I stood throwing rocks into the deserted pasture, a dark unease filled me. I always looked forward to these times of spending the night in Pa-Pa's old farmhouse, where the loud ticking of the clock on the mantle in his bedroom, just down the hall from my room, lulled me to sleep.

For some reason today felt much different. An unusual homesickness filled me, even though my home was only eight miles southwest of my grandfather's home and I had only left my parents thirty minutes earlier.

While I was trying to deal with my emotions, my father suddenly appeared around the corner of the store and parked near the steps. A tremendous relief overwhelmed me as I ran to the car.

"What're you doin' here?" I asked.

My father smiled weakly as he opened the car door. "We just heard another high school student in town came down with infantile paralysis." Looking down at me somberly, Daddy continued, "You know how your mother is. She wants you home where she can keep an eye on you."

Even though he had thrown the concern onto my mother, I could tell Daddy would also be relieved to have me home. During that seasonal outbreak of the polio virus, parents were terribly fearful for their children. In the 2020 coronavirus outbreak, the concern has switched, of course, as children are most fearful for their parents.

Back in the 1940s and early 1950s—before Jonas Salk came up with a vaccine in 1955—parents were petrified that their children would come down with the dreaded disease, which could cripple or paralyze for life. In extreme cases, children had to be placed in an iron lung in order to breathe.

I remember how with the slightest crick in my neck, Mother would go into a panic. Now, polio is virtually wiped out all over the globe and a child's stiff neck is once again just a stiff neck.

That palpable fear, as always, filtered down to us children. Surely that explained why I was feeling homesick earlier. Home was where I felt most safe during this time of fear and high anxiety.

As with the coronavirus, the virus causing polio could not be seen, but we knew it was always lurking. There were no masks, but social distancing was common. Swimming pools were all empty since the polio virus seemed to thrive in water.

Albert Sabin's oral vaccine replaced Jonas Salk's vaccine in the 1960s. I remember how common areas were set up in my hometown of Mt. Gilead, where families would receive the oral vaccine by way of a cube of sweet-tasting substance—almost like a sugar cube.

The first public oral polio vaccination I can remember receiving was in the shop/agricultural building next to our local high school. It was a strange feeling to fall in line with a large group of people whom we had previously been carefully avoiding.

As a result of that vaccine, the fear of polio has, thankfully, passed. We know, too, that the coronavirus will one day be mostly wiped out and those fears will also be in the past. In the meantime, we practice caution—especially social distancing. I don't like it any better today than I did as a young boy. But, again, we do it because it is necessary—and caring.

I find it difficult to understand why people resent wearing a mask if it keeps someone from contracting a disease with the potential to kill. At the heart of Jesus's teaching is the expectation to "love my neighbor as myself."

But I was thinking the other day how ironic it is that one of the primary answers to combating the coronavirus is keeping a safe distance from each other, while the answer to our spiritual and emotional needs is snuggling in as close to God as we can get.

Grace opens the door into an intimate relationship with God in spite of our spiritual sicknesses, weaknesses, limitations, wrong-heartedness, and voluntary separation. And there, in that intimate togetherness, our deepest hurts are healed.

So we ask God to help us endure our present separation from those we love and desperately want to hug. Well, not just endure but emerge better on the other side: "We also glory in our sufferings, because we know that suffering produces perseverance; perseverance, character; and character, hope. And hope does not put us to shame, because God's love has been poured out into our hearts through the Holy Spirit, who has been given to us" (Rom 5:3–5).

On the journey to Mullinix, we will pass many things, and many things will pass us. But by God's grace we will be better for all the passings.

God willing, before long we will be able to hug each other so tightly that it will be difficult to breathe.

# Part Five

A Breathtaking Journey

Is Full of Interesting Critters

# Long-Haired Ringbearer

"May the grace of God be upon you."

The retired Lutheran pastor, who was my officiating partner in this wedding ceremony, spoke in a well-seasoned, resonant voice. "And also with you," the 150-plus family and friends responded with enthusiasm.

Their enthusiasm was impressive given the presence of dark, threatening clouds moving over the wedding venue, on top of a steep knoll looking toward the distant blue haze of the Blue Ridge Mountains.

Suddenly the clouds were no longer threatening but were in full attack mode as the first sprinkles began falling on the bridal party and guests. The string orchestra grew silent as the musicians quickly placed their expensive instruments in their cases and sprinted toward shelter.

The bride's father, escorting his lovely daughter down the aisle, turned to the guests and said, "This is much too quiet. Can anyone hum?" Everyone immediately began humming "Here Comes the Bride," growing louder and louder as their confidence in their humming ability accelerated.

But just as we began the ceremony, the wedding planner came running down the slick, grassy aisle, grabbed the full skirt of the flowing wedding dress, and shouted to the bride, "We've got to go!"

Many in the wedding party began walking rapidly or racing down the slippery hill, depending on physical ability or their degree of pride in maintaining a modicum of dignity. Dignity is hard to maintain in a driving rain, no matter how well-dressed one might be.

I had ridden up the hill to the wedding venue on a shuttle bus with the bridesmaids. (I have picked up a number of helpful hints from performing weddings for more than fifty years. Bridesmaids seem to have the most fun and always smell better.) But as I waited in line to board the bus for the return trip, I was certain I was getting more drenched than if I had casually strolled down the hill.

Finally, we all stood dripping in the lodge—a converted birthing barn on the lush, expansive Mt. Ida Farm, a few miles outside Charlottesville, Virginia. Expensive hairdos hung in scraggly ringlets or plastered to wet faces. Dripping, pricey dresses were forming large puddles of water on the concrete floor of the smaller of two rooms selected by the wedding planner to continue the ceremony.

My heart went out to the bride and groom and their families who had evidently spent a sizable sum of money to make everything perfect. I soon discovered, however, that my empathy was not needed.

As I took my place beside the Lutheran minister, I looked up and was surprised to see everyone smiling. These were not plastered-on, fake smiles, but genuine tooth-baring smiles. I didn't see a frown in the entire assembly. Instead, there was the happy camaraderie that often occurs when a group of people have overcome adversity together.

Sometimes the worst brings out the worst in us, so it's a happy event when the worst brings out the best.

Strangers began helping each other. Blow dryers were shared. A woman's heel on her expensive shoes disintegrated from being waterlogged for so long. Seeing that, one of the caterer's employees reached into her bag and brought out a new pair of flip-flops, still attached by a plastic ring, and offered them to the limping, heelless woman.

Then, as the procession began again in this newly adapted venue, the smiles grew wider and quiet comments were exchanged over how good everyone looked even soaking wet.

After the ceremony I asked one of the groomsmen how his hair was so quickly restored to its former thickness and shape. "Oh," he said smiling widely, "I just went into the bathroom and rubbed my head down with a paper towel."

There are some advantages to being young, in addition to the absence of arthritis. Good hair is one of them.

The ceremony was now resuming in its predictable fashion. After officiating at over 400 weddings, I was finding them so predictable that I was becoming a little bored with the whole affair. On Thursday of the week before my wife and I left for Charlottesville, I had expressed those sentiments to a friend, adding, "I don't think I can be surprised anymore. I've seen so many attempts to be different that even the changes look the same."

My mind was suddenly jerked back to the present as my colleague was asking the best man for the rings. Almost frantically, the bride whispered, "You're supposed to ask for the ringbearer to come forward." Realizing his mistake, the retired Lutheran pastor said, "Will the ringbearer please bring the rings."

All of us looked up as a young girl burst through the door. However, our eyes did not remain on her long as our attention was immediately drawn to the little dog at the end of a decorative leash she held in her right hand.

The long-haired dachshund, dressed in a formal black tuxedo, ran excitedly into the crowd to his left, then across the aisle to his right. Turning to the guests, the bride explained apologetically, "He's been practicing outdoors."

After the splendidly attired canine was retrieved and set at the top of the aisle, he ran swiftly toward his beloved owner and jumped into her arms, smothering her with kisses.

When the handsome groom kissed his new wife at the end of the ceremony, it was no contest. The long-haired dachshund was far more passionate. In all fairness to Alex, however, I have always discouraged the groom from extravagant licking of the bride's lips and eyes and ears and cheeks in a public setting. Long-haired dachshunds, even one with such a distinguished name as Winston, don't understand proper decorum and must be forgiven. Chuckling to myself, I muttered, "Well, I guess there are still surprises to be had."

Later during the ceremony, I had an opportunity to thank Cameron for inviting me to participate in her wedding. I had accepted the invitation primarily because of my approximately forty-five years of conducting weddings and funerals for her family. In fact, I had joined Cameron's parents in marriage thirty years prior, so I was happy for the chance to continue my longtime relationship with this fine family.

I talked about how, through all the highs and lows, the times of grieving and the times of celebrating, I had watched Cameron's extended family walk together with strength, compassion, and grace.

I then reflected on how this event—ripe with the potential of washing away the dreams of a beautiful wedding—had instead become a place where grace was once again displayed in its full grandeur.

As the rain had begun to fall and we made a mad dash for cover, Alex and Cameron took a brief but poignant moment to turn to each other with a smile and say, "Well, we tried." And they had. As the radar had shown a line of rain-laden clouds approaching, they had persisted.

Riding in the backseat of a car down the knoll toward cover, Cameron glanced back at the rose-covered trellis, now almost invisible through the driving rain, and asked, "Mother, am I still getting married? Nothing matters but marrying Alex."

It's always impressive when someone can hold on to priorities in the face of a crisis.

Cameron's mother, Beth, assured her that the marriage would certainly take place. Secretly, Beth could not help but be a little pleased that she and her husband, Brian, had one more chance to "fix a mess" for their little girl before she became a married woman.

When our best efforts have failed, the best thing we can do is meet the crumbling dreams with the grace that transforms broken plans into new plans.

Promises are too easily broken these days. Experiences of grace bind us with cords that are much more difficult to be ripped apart than simple words.

I thanked Cameron that I could be a part of all that. I also thanked her for the wonderful surprise of a long-haired dachshund ringbearer. It offers hope that after all these years of performing weddings, I can still anticipate more surprises.

After all, we do serve a God of surprises.

And there were shepherds living out in the fields nearby, keeping watch over their flocks at night. An angel of the Lord appeared to them, and the glory of the Lord shone around them, and they were terrified. But the angel said to them, "Do not be afraid. I bring you good news that will cause great joy for all the people. Today in the town of David a Savior has been born to you; he is the Messiah, the Lord." (Luke 2:8–11)

The lives of those dirty, smelly shepherds were transformed forever by the breathtaking surprise of a bright light in the middle of a dark night.

Thank you, Cameron and Alex, for showing us once again the power of love to bring joy even in the presence of a raging storm.

# The Fish Beneath My Feet

I was leisurely talking with my father when a swirling disturbance stopped us both in mid-sentence. Remembering the string of crappie I had caught and hung off the pier, I reached down and jerked the heavy string of fish out of the water.

The shadowy outline of a large fish followed the line of crappie to the surface—mouth open to snatch a helpless victim for his lunch.

"That's a largemouth bass," I yelled to my father, who was standing on the bank beside the pier. Hastily, I removed the night crawler and small hook from the swivel. I knew neither was strong enough to catch this fish, which dwarfed the ones I had caught in the previous hour.

After placing a broken-back minnow lure on my line, I began casting out into the creek toward the river. Out of the corner of my eye, I saw my father hastily ready his rod and reel to get in on the action.

The pier on which I was standing extended into a little inlet on the left side of my parents' cabin, constructed of wide oak boards that seemed to grow stronger each year. The main body of Little River ran in front of the cabin and along the right side, creating a small private peninsula for our family's getaway.

Two, three, four times, I cast as far as I could with no strike from the large bass. "Drop it down by the pier," my father said. My father grew up along this river and knew about fishing. Releasing the reel, I dropped the lure into the water just beneath my feet. No sooner did it disappear from my sight than I felt a sudden violent pull.

"Got 'im!" I yelled to my father. But as I tried to reel the bass in and lift him out of the water, it became obvious that my small rod was no match for the weight of this fish. To add to my dilemma, I had no net since the size of the fish I normally caught required nothing more than a gentle lift and the fish landed on the pier.

While I was puzzling over what to do next, my father called out, "Play him around in a circle until he comes by the bank, and I'll catch him." Through the years my father had told me stories of seining for fish with a large net in preparation for a church fish fry. Occasionally, he would describe how he and his brothers would catch fish by hand, so I trusted his knowledge and experience.

Miraculously, following my father's instructions, I was able to swing the fish in ever-widening circles, nearer and nearer the bank where my father stood waiting. Finally, he reached down and, with one swoop, grabbed the bass under the gills, pulling him out of the water.

I was astounded at both my father's skill and the size of the fish. Now, as far as fish go, this eight-pounder certainly set no records, but it was by far the largest fish I had caught at that time.

*Still Going to Mullinix*

Many years later, while fishing with Brent, my youngest grandson, who was twelve years old at the time, I watched him pull a ten-pound catfish from the Powhatan Creek along the James River. "Well, Son," I said, "it took me thirty-some years to catch an eight-pounder. So don't let catching this ten-pounder during your twelfth year make all your other catches anticlimactic. There's always a bigger one out there."

My Uncle Branson, who spent a large portion of his retirement fishing, took one look at that bass, which we had temporarily placed in a little pond at my parents' home, and said, "Jerry, I know how you fish. You better have that one mounted."

On my next birthday, my parents presented me with the bass mounted on a dark walnut board. It still hangs in my home study.

The only downside to this whole episode was the disappointment of my four-year-old son, Brian, who reluctantly informed me with one of the saddest faces I have ever seen on a young boy: "Daddy, you didn't catch that fish."

"What do you mean?" I asked, surprised.

"Granddaddy caught it," he concluded with unusual certainty for a four-year-old.

Brian, Brent's father, is now in his mid-forties, but I think he still believes my daddy caught that fish. Well, no matter who caught it, that long-ago experience taught me a valuable lesson that I don't always follow.

I have noticed that most of us seem to think the best of everything is "out there"—at least somewhere I am not. Although I had seen the bass right beneath my feet, my first instinct was to cast away from the pier. I have also noticed that when I'm on the bank, I cast as far out into the river as I can. But when I'm out in the middle of the river in Daddy's jon boat, I cast as near to the bank as I can. Surely the biggest fish is "out there" or "over there"—not here.

I've witnessed that same pattern in countless lives over the years.

When I was a very young pastor, I had an older mentor, the lead pastor of the Williamsburg Methodist Church, whom I had asked to lead our church in the study of a somewhat specialized topic. He kindly refused, telling me, "My church is just down the road. Take it from my years of experience. Your people will listen more carefully to someone from out of town. An expert is anyone who is not from here."

I argued with him, but subsequent years have proven the wisdom of his advice.

The best is always out there. The best spouse, the best house, the best job, the best teacher, the best preacher—always out there. Never here. So we end up in a constant state of restless discontent.

I had a good friend in the first church I served who surprised me one day with the sudden news: "Well, I just wanted to let you know that we're moving in a month."

To say I was startled is an understatement. During lunch the previous week, he had told me how happy he was with his job and his family—a wife and two children. So I asked, "What happened? Did you get fired?"

"Oh, no," he replied, laughing. "I have to move every three years or I get so cranky that my family can't stand me."

"Why three years?" I asked.

"Don't know," he said. "That just seems to be the time I need a change."

I kept persisting. I hated to lose his friendship, but I also could not understand his restless desire for something different. "What are you looking for that you don't have right where you are?"

My friend paused for several minutes with a deep frown on his face before answering. "I don't know," he said. "I can't put my finger on it, but I always feel that something better is out there."

A month later, he and his family packed up and moved to a distant state. I never saw them again.

A few weeks after my friend's departure, I was working on a sermon and came across Paul's prayer for the Ephesians: "I pray that out of his glorious riches he may strengthen you with power through his Spirit in your inner being, so that Christ may dwell in your hearts through faith. And I pray that you, being rooted and established in love..." (Eph 3:16–17).

Maybe being "rooted and grounded in love" means discovering that our real roots lie in discovering the meaning and joy of life in our "inner being." Could our failure to make a home in our hearts for Christ be the reason for our restless longing for something "out there"?

Every once in a while, I still hear my father's quiet voice saying, "Stop casting way out there, Son. Drop your line right where you're standing."

It's kind of breathtaking to realize that it still works today.

# Ducks from Duck Eggs

On almost every trip to visit my parents in my hometown of Mt. Gilead, North Carolina, the ducks populating my father's fishpond have either reminded me of an old truth or taught me a new lesson. My lesson on this particular trip came by way of my five-year-old nephew, Benjamin, my brother Kent's son.

Benjamin lived just across the pond from my parents' home and met me almost as soon as I crawled out of the car following the five-hour drive from my home in Williamsburg, Virginia. He was aware that I shared his interest in all God's critters and had some exciting news he was bursting to tell.

"Uncle Jerry!" he cried while grabbing my hand and guiding me to the far side of the pond nearest his home. "Granddaddy put some duck eggs under a chicken!" Hurriedly, he explained how the duck that had laid the eggs had been killed by a night predator sneaking through the darkness. "So Grandaddy found a settin' hen and put the duck eggs under *it*!" At every word, his eyes widened with incredulity.

When we arrived at the nest, the prospective mother chicken expressed her displeasure at our intrusion by clucking angrily. Benjamin paid no attention as he gently lifted her aside.

"See?" he asked excitedly. "Those bigger eggs are the duck eggs!" Sure enough, there were several oval chicken eggs interspersed with approximately a half dozen larger, more elongated duck eggs.

The pleasure in his eyes was evident as he continued his narrative: "And you know what Granddaddy said?" I waited expectantly as we stepped back to allow the agitated hen to resume her place on the nest. Continuing in his high-pitched, five-year-old voice, Benjamin exclaimed, "Granddaddy said those duck eggs are *still* going to be little ducks!"

"Even though a chicken is hatching them?" I exclaimed.

"Yep," Benjamin replied, pleased at my dumbfounded look. "All those duck eggs are *still* going to be baby ducks!"

I shook my head in wonder while muttering, "Amazing! Hard to imagine." That seemed to please Benjamin greatly, as we turned to retrace our steps around the north end of the pond to answer my parents' question as to why my car was parked in their backyard but the driver was nowhere to be seen.

I thought of Benjamin and those duck eggs again the other day as I reread the story of Jesus's emotional lament to the inhabitants of Jerusalem: "'Jerusalem, Jerusalem, you who kill the prophets and stone those sent to you, how often I have longed to gather your children together, as a hen gathers her chicks under her wings, and you were not willing'" (Luke 13:34).

Now, I'm not at all surprised at how passionately Jesus calls out to the wandering folks in Jerusalem. The entire biblical story, as I understand it, is about a loving God seeking to bring us home to himself. But the truly astounding thing is that when we crawl under Jesus's wings as one thing, unlike Benjamin's duck eggs, we emerge as something entirely different.

Nicodemus had trouble understanding that too. Oh, he had heard of Jesus's teachings and wondered about them—especially this one: "'Very truly I tell you, no one can see the kingdom of God unless they are born again'" (John 3:3).

Nicodemus's response seems to drip with sarcasm: "'How can someone be born when they are old?' Nicodemus asked. 'Surely they cannot enter a second time into their mother's womb to be born!'" (John 3:4).

Of course that can't be done. Nicodemus is right. But even if such a thing were possible, it wouldn't change anything. Nicodemus would still be Nicodemus and no doubt during late middle age would become a Pharisee and church council member just as surely as ducks always come from duck eggs.

But then the wind started blowing, and Jesus saw another opportunity to draw a lesson from the natural world: "'The wind blows wherever it pleases. You hear its sound, but you cannot tell where it comes from or where it is going. So it is with everyone born of the Spirit'" (John 3:8).

Nicodemus appears to be fairly intelligent and begins to realize that maybe the spirit of God acting on his heart *could* bring about a radical change. If only he accepted the invitation to hide under the wings of the living Son of God, Nicodemus could emerge as something entirely different.

Looks like it actually happened. After Jesus's crucifixion, Nicodemus went with Joseph of Arimathea to take possession of the body of Jesus and prepare it for burial according to Jewish customs (John 19:38–40).

I'm sure your granddaddy is right, Benjamin: Ducks will emerge from those duck eggs even though they are being hatched by a chicken. Those little ones will still quack like ducks, walk like ducks, and look like ducks.

But when we crawl under the wings of the inviting Christ, we are hatched into something entirely different—true children of God. Nicodemus no longer walked like Nicodemus, talked like Nicodemus, or looked like Nicodemus.

Benjamin, that's when my eyes become as large as yours and my breath comes in the same excited gasps at the sheer wonder of it all.

# Cute Bathing Suits and Killer Whales

I had an uneasy feeling of impending doom as I watched two small children lead their smiling father down to the first row of the "splash zone." My fears for this little family were soon dramatically realized.

On our way home to Williamsburg, Virginia, from officiating at a wedding in Key West, Florida, I persuaded my wife to stop at Sea World in Orlando. Jean doesn't share my passion for sea life or critters of most kinds. Clouds and birds are her thing. But she agreed to indulge me.

After marveling at all the fascinating creatures in the huge aquariums, I suggested we catch the next show in the Shamu theater of the killer whales. Recent events have caused Sea World to phase out this portion of their attractions, but when we were there in 2005, the Orca killer whales were the premier attraction. I did not want to miss them.

We noticed that the first fourteen rows in front of the theater were designated the "splash zone." We decided to sit in the fourteenth row—thinking we could handle a little splatter without getting completely drenched.

As we were taking our seats, two excited children entered with their proud father clinging to their tiny hands. It was obvious from his smug look that he knew how cute his offspring looked, "chips off the old block," in their bright swimsuits with smiles to match.

Glancing sympathetically toward us scaredy-cat old folks sitting so far from the action, the cute kids eagerly pulled their father down the center steps, passing row after row until they plopped down, full of confidence, in the very first row. "Not a good idea," I muttered to Jean.

Soon, however, I became totally engrossed in the antics of those massive Orcas responding obediently to the directions of their trainers. In my semi-trance, I had forgotten all about those enthusiastic children in their cute bathing suits. That is, until the first blood-curdling scream pierced the "ooohs" and "aahhhs" of the crowd and reached our ears with frightful clarity all the way back in the fourteenth row.

One of the killer whales had flamboyantly leaped onto the platform immediately in front of the young family, splashing its huge tail toward the two children. It wasn't the largest splash of the day—just a medium-size one, really. But it was enough to swamp the pretty blonde girl whose carefully coiffured curly hair now hung in limp, dripping strands. Her younger brother jumped up, frantically wiping the water out of his eyes with both hands—soaked as thoroughly as his sister.

This traumatic, unexpected turn of events jettisoned both children out into the aisle, frantically dragging their father—a sheepish grin now replacing his smug smile—back up past the splash zone to the safety of the exit at the top of the steps.

By the time they reached us in the fourteenth row, the children's terror had become too deeply felt for noise as their little mouths stretched into round, soundless circles, so large that their faces were no longer distinguishable. Their bright eyes had disappeared into the folds of their straining red cheeks in an unintended but quite accurate impersonation of Charlie Brown.

Near the top of the steps, the young father bent to lift his children into his arms, their feet now dragging as they struggled to walk on shock-weakened legs. I wondered if the embarrassed smile on the father's face was because of the uproar his children were making or from a sense of failure at protecting them from such a traumatic experience.

I've been there as a father. But those children were so eager to go down front that I couldn't blame this father for wanting to grant their wishes. I've been there too.

My primary thoughts, however, were on the stark contrast between the confident exuberance of the children in their cute bathing suits entering the theater with such high expectations and their complete devastation upon exiting in abject fear.

Experiences often do not fulfill our expectations.

However, the place of unrealized expectations is also where some of our best lessons are learned. Those two traumatized children will not soon forget the lesson from that day: Cute bathing suits are no match for killer whales.

The Mullinix journey toward realizing the full potential of the person I was created to be is filled with threatening whales eagerly poised to drown my expectations under volumes of water.

I guess all this means, at the very least, is that I should pay more attention to Paul's advice to the church at Ephesus: "Put on the full armor of God, so that you can take your stand against the devil's schemes" (Eph 6:11).

Those panicked children pop into my mind from time to time, and I have to chuckle. But they also remind me of the silly, woefully inadequate things in which we try to clothe ourselves as protection against the dangers of this world. Only the armor of "truth, righteousness, peace, faith, and prayer" are sufficient.

The huge attacks from the killer whales of this world are enough to take my breath away—just as it did those unsuspecting children. But, thank God, it is just as breathtaking to know that there is armor enough for my protection—just waiting for me to slip it on.

# A Largemouth Mama's Wisdom

It was turning out to be one of those days. The weather was perfect, the water was calm, and the laughter was contagious. The only problem was we were unable to hook any of the fish that were skillfully stealing the fat night crawlers from our hooks.

Finally, my twelve-year-old grandson snagged a fish that was scarcely larger than a minnow. Swinging the tiny fish toward me, Brent said, laughing, "Here, Papa, you like sardines."

He is right, of course. To the disgust of some members of my family, I do enjoy sardines—especially when they are drowned in a pool of vinegar. W. D. Edwards, a friend over in Saluda, offered the very helpful tip that the King Oscar brand of sardines is the best. He was right. Delicious.

Going along with Brent's joke, I laid my rod and reel on the pier between us, leaving it unsecured as I grabbed for my sardine. If this was the size of fish biting today, what could possibly go wrong?

Of course, that's the way it is with fishing. You never know when the big one is going to strike. Unfortunately, this big one struck just as I had removed my hand from the rod now lying unattended on the pier.

With no warning, the rod and all the tackle attached to it jettisoned off the end of the pier, quickly sinking into the murky water. It all happened so fast that neither Brent nor I had a chance to react as we helplessly watched our oldest, but still one of our favorite, rod and reel disappear with only a few bubbles indicating its rapid movement down Powhatan Creek.

Brent and I looked at each other in stunned silence before bursting into uncontrollable laughter. After catching his breath, Brent said, "We didn't even have time to reach for it."

"No," I replied. "The way he took off, he had to be a large bass."

After we had both expressed our disappointment at not having a chance to catch him, I said, "Can you imagine the scene at the front door of the fish hut when he returns home?"

"Probably the oldest son out looking for food for the family," Brent said, as our imaginations took wing.

"Yeah," I replied, "probably ran up to the front door hollering for his mama, all excited. 'Mama! Mama! Look at the big worm I just caught.'" Worms are terrestrial, so the largemouth son had not seen many in his water world. His diet had consisted mostly of small fish, with the occasional crayfish and large insects thrown in for crunchy protein snacks. This land-dwelling worm was a rare treat.

Mama Largemouth Bass looked at her largemouth son over her large spectacles and said, "Law, chile, you have to spit that worm out before I can see it. Open that large mouth and let Mama see."

But before the largemouth elder son could open his large mouth, his mama caught herself on the door frame as she fell backwards in a half-faint. "Wait! Wait! What in the world is that you're dragging behind you?"

"I'm not sure, Mama," the largemouth son said, shrugging his large gills as he looked back at the rod and reel. "It followed me all the way home. I kept swimming faster and faster—even did a few of my go-to fancy moves that always fool my schoolmates—but I couldn't shake it."

Pausing to take a large breath, the largemouth son opened his large mouth for his largemouth mama to remove the hook and continued, "This delicious fat worm was hanging on the end of a line, and when I grabbed it, that strange thing leaped into the water and chased me all the way home. I guess it was as hungry as I was. Surely didn't want to let go of that worm."

The mother largemouth had finally regained her composure and explained, "Son, you just had a close call."

"I did?" the elder son exclaimed in surprise.

"Yep," his mother replied. "Usually when you grab a worm at the end of that contraption, it will jerk you out of the water."

*Still Going to Mullinix*

"Out of the water?" the largemouth son cried, his large face growing pale. "I—I couldn't breathe if I was out of the water!" In fact, the very thought took his breath away.

"That's why you were so lucky," his mama replied. Then, much softer, she continued, "It happened to me once."

"What did you do?" her son asked. This was something completely new to him.

"Well," the mama largemouth said, a single tear sliding down her top left gill and disappearing into its depths, "I was lucky too. After being jerked out of the water, I landed so hard on a wooden pier that it took my breath away."

The largemouth son listened with his large mouth wide open, fearing for his mother's life.

"But then," his mother continued quietly, "I discovered that it wasn't the pier that knocked the breath out of me. It was that I had no water for my gills to absorb oxygen."

"Then how did you survive? Why are you here now?" her largemouth son asked anxiously.

"That was the lucky part," his mother replied with a large smile spreading across her large mouth. "The young fisherman who pulled me out of the water had a kind heart."

"What do you mean?" her largemouth son asked, wishing his largemouth mother would hurry her story along.

"Well, the two fishermen gently hung me on what they called a 'scale,' and the man, whom the young fisherman called 'Papa,' cried, 'Wow! Almost eight pounds!' I was wriggling and struggling to breathe, but I took offense at that. I had never weighed that much in my whole life and decided right then and there to cut down on some of those fat frogs I so enjoy for lunch!"

"But, Mother, you were trying to survive! How could you even think about your weight?"

"I know, I know," the largemouth mama said as she looked lovingly at her young son. She had a large mother's heart. "You're right smart, Son, but you still have a lot to learn about girl fish."

His mother chuckled at her largemouth son's puzzled look as she continued with her story. "Then, just when I thought I had breathed my last, the young fisherman who had pulled me out of the water said, 'Hurry and get him back in the water, Papa! We don't want him to die.' Bless his heart. Guess he couldn't tell I was a girl."

Another large, tender tear slid down the largemouth mama's right top gill at the memory of the young fisherman's kindness. "So just when I was sure I had breathed my last, I hit the water with a large splash and took a large breath as the lifegiving water flowed through my gills."

The largemouth son suddenly discovered he was holding his own breath as he listened, enthralled.

"So I'm here today because of the kindness of a young human. But," she added hastily, "let me warn you, Son. Not all humans are that way." Two more large tears slid down her large mouth as she continued, "I had a large younger brother who was jerked out of the water and never seen again."

The largemouth son's large eyes grew even larger as he tried to imagine the sadness of it all.

"Humans are just like fish," the mother largemouth continued. "Some are kind, and that kindness will give you a happy life. Others are very unkind, and that unkindness can take your happiness away."

"But in class the other day," the largemouth son interrupted, "Teacher showed us pictures of the brains of different kinds of animals. The brains of humans looked much larger than ours. They should be smart enough not to be unkind."

"Oh, honey," the largemouth mother said, "it isn't the size of the brain that matters. It's the size of the heart."

The largemouth son's eyes were large with confusion. "But how do you know the size of a heart?"

"That's the hard part," his mother replied, shaking her large head sadly. "You can't just listen to their words. Humans can be very deceitful. They lie a lot."

"Then how do you see the heart?" the largemouth son persisted, growing a little impatient.

"Well," his largemouth mother said, leaning back in her large rocker and beginning to rock slowly. "You have to watch them for a long time. Find some clear water on a cloudy day so the sun won't blind you. Then watch how the humans treat each other."

"How long will that take?" the largemouth son replied with a large pout beginning to form around his large mouth. "Teacher said we only live to about fifteen years or so. Is that enough time to watch?" Ever since his largemouth teacher had told the class about their expected life span, he had been worried about not having enough time to do the important things. His grandfather had lived for twenty years, but that was so unusual that they still talked about it down at the sushi bar.

His largemouth mother gave a large laugh. "Oh, Son, it doesn't matter how many days you live. What matters is how you fill those days."

"Fill them with what?" the largemouth son asked with a large frown. Life seemed to be getting awfully complicated.

"Noticing, honey," his largemouth mama explained. "Noticing carefully all the little and big things humans do to each other. Are they generous and considerate—always putting the other person first?" The largemouth mama paused for a moment before adding, "Actually, Son, you might not have to watch very long because the true heart can't be hidden. Sooner or later—usually sooner—kindness or unkindness will reveal itself. It just naturally bursts out from the heart."

The largemouth son was happy to learn all this, but now he was getting impatient. His largemouth teacher had told his mother that she felt he lacked a large attention span. Called it ADHD—whatever that meant. It sounded like a dreadful disease, but so far he hadn't developed any rashes on his large stomach. He also heard the largemouth teacher tell his mama that it happened more to boy fish than girl fish. His largemouth teacher was always taking up for the largemouth girls.

But now he knew what he had to do and flipped over into a large dive. "Wait!" his largemouth mother hollered. "Where are you going in such a hurry?"

"I'm going to take the rod and reel back where I found it dangling off the pier at the end of our creek. You know, where that man with one black dog and one white dog lives. The white dog likes to come down to the pier and watch. I think I heard the young fisherman call him 'Uncle Chris.'"

"Oh, yes," the mama largemouth said, nodding her head. "I know him. Generous fellow, seems like. Always having folks over to swim in his pool. But remember what I told you. Swim quickly out of our front yard when he rides by with his boat on his way to the James River. Wouldn't intentionally run you over, I'm sure, but as soon as he comes to the head of the creek, he really guns it."

"That's the place," the largemouth son said. "So I thought the kind thing would be to throw that contraption that followed me home back onto the pier."

His mother gave a large nod of her large head and laughed, "Yes, that is the kind thing to do, but you are not strong enough to throw it out of the water onto the pier."

"I'm stronger than all my large friends," the largemouth son said while flipping his large tail and flexing his large gills.

"That's true," his largemouth mother agreed. "But even if you succeeded in throwing it onto the pier, the two fishermen would probably die of shock—especially the large one."

After thinking about it for a few minutes, the largemouth son agreed. "You're probably right." He gave a large frown of disappointment, but then a large smile suddenly filled his large face as a large idea came to him. "Maybe next time I'll just slip the worm off gently and not get snagged on the hook."

"That's a good idea," his largemouth mother said. "We've been doing that for generations. It's a lot of fun. And I think the fishermen enjoy it too because they start hollering and stomping and even invent words I've never heard before." Mama largemouth paused to make sure her largemouth son was listening. "But it's risky, Son, and takes a large amount of skill."

The largemouth son's large eyes grew even larger as he swam away with another large flip of his large tail. "Oh," he cried over his left gills, "I got skills! I got skills!"

The largemouth mother felt a large amount of both pride and worry as she watched her son swim out of sight. But isn't that the way with all mothers—large or small?

"The end!" Brent suddenly exclaimed.

I laughed and agreed the story had gone on long enough.

Brent and I rested our imaginations and chuckled over our story as we joined Blue, Uncle Chris's white dog, who was eagerly watching the red and white bobbers dance in the calm water.

Finally, Brent said, "Papa, wouldn't it be fun if all of that really could have happened?"

I smiled and leaned back into a more comfortable position on my blue fishing chair. "I've lived a long time, good buddy, and seen a lot of surprising things. It's a mysterious world where all kinds of unexpected things happen."

Brent nodded as I concluded, "But one thing I know for sure: If things are going to work out at all in this crazy world, we all have to show a lot more kindness toward each other—both under the water and on top of the water."

Brent gave a short laugh as he reached for the can of worms. "You're right there, Papa. But right now I wish some kind fish would take a big bite of my bait."

I watched Brent slip another worm onto the hook and idly wondered about his future. I know he has a large heart, so I have hope that at least the part of the world Brent touches will somehow be made better by his kindness.

I guess that's pretty much the way most change happens—one person at a time showing kindness in the part of the world he or she touches. Seems we often give up because the job appears too large—even overwhelming. Transformation of the whole, however, always seems to come one piece at a time. Surely we can handle that.

"Get the net, Papa! Get the net! I've got a big one!" Brent suddenly shouted. As I grabbed for the net, the thought flashed through my mind, "Sometimes good things do happen at unexpected times."

Those are the special moments that always take my breath away.

# Part Six

A Breathtaking Journey

Encounters Intriguing People

# Just Call Me Ed

I love characters. Those people who look a little differently, act a little differently, and see life a little differently intrigue me. Rarely do I let an opportunity to talk to such individuals pass.

So when I stopped by the Rite Aid on John Tyler Highway to pick up a prescription the other day and saw a man with a bushy red and gray beard and a still thick head of matching hair partially covered by a biker's cap, I knew I had to find out more about him. The biker's cap certainly was appropriate since the man was leaning against a huge Harley-Davidson in the parking spot closest to the store entrance.

His wrinkled face, obviously weather-beaten from miles spent on the road in the sun and rushing wind, was partially hidden behind the thick plumes of smoke rising from the cigarette he held in his right hand.

Climbing out of my car, I walked over and nodded toward his bike. "How many miles you got on it?"

"Not many miles on this 'un," he replied hesitantly, his wary eyes carefully looking me over.

"New?" I asked.

"Kinda," he replied, taking a long drag on his cigarette. "Had a lot on m' ol' 'un."

"Did a lot of traveling?"

He nodded slowly before explaining, "Been goin' t' California ever' summer for twenty-six year."

I caught myself before asking if he traveled with a gang. Sounded too much like profiling. So instead I said, "Who do you go with?" Before he could answer, I said, "By the way, my name is Jerry Haywood."

That little bit of information was obviously quite boring to him as he continued to draw on his cigarette and stare blankly. Then, exhaling another thick cloud of dark smoke, he finally grunted, "Just call m' Ed."

I nodded, smiling, before repeating my question. "So who do you travel with?"

"Nobody," Ed replied, a little more friendly. "By m'self."

"All the way across country on a bike by yourself!" I exclaimed, trying to sound as impressed as I was.

"Yep," he said, sounding totally unimpressed. But I could sense he was willing—and maybe as eager as he ever got about anything—to tell me more.

"Does your family worry about you?" I asked, hoping he had someone somewhere who cared.

"Call 'em ever' day on the road," Ed replied, not bothering to explain who "they" were. I was definitely not going to push my luck by getting too personal.

Following a moment of silence, which I filled by looking down at his bike and he filled by lighting another cigarette, I asked, "Do you camp out or stay in motels?"

Warming a little to me and our conversation, Ed said, "Stay 'n motels. Start look'n' for a place 'round three in th' afternoon." He took a few more drags on his cigarette before adding, "Some folks got so's they look for me 'long th' way."

"That's good," I said, as if he would care about my opinion. "I expect a warm bed feels good after hours on the Harley."

Ed nodded slowly as he answered, "Yep. Agent Orange's killin' m' legs. Now start'n' to feel it in m' hips."

I nodded sympathetically before saying, "I have a good friend who's suffering for the same reason. He can hardly walk now."

"All of us'n who spent time in Vietnam begin to feel it one way or 'nother. 'Specially since I turned seventy a coupla years back."

Ed looked much older than seventy-two, but riding cross-country on a Harley-Davidson for twenty-six years could certainly account for that. "How long were you in the military?" I asked. I felt I was pushing his patience by asking so many questions. And I have never liked nosiness—or small talk, for that matter. But, like I said, characters intrigue me.

Ed took another long drag on his cigarette and let his eyes search back through the years before answering, "Jus' three year. But Vietnam made it feel like thirty." He looked up, and his eyes were obviously remembering a painful past full of things he would rather forget.

In an effort to steer our conversation back to the present, I said, "I bet you've seen a lot of things riding across this big country."

A hint of a smile played at the corners of Ed's mouth as he replied, "Yep, lotsa things. Good 'n bad." Again, he looked down as memories paraded through his mind.

It was obvious he was not wanting to share those stories, so I simply said, "I sure would like to have some of those experiences."

Ed looked terribly indifferent as he barely nodded. It was obvious he was finished with this idle chatter.

"Well," I said, turning toward the front door of Rite Aid, "guess I better get on in and get my prescription. Nice talking to you." Ed took my extended hand. His grip was firm.

He had been silent when I shook his rough right hand, but as I opened the drugstore door, he called out, "Hey, buddy."

"Yeah?"

"Know how ya c'n have that exper'ence?"

"How's that?" I asked, holding the door open as I turned toward him.

Ed nodded down at his bike as he said, "Get ya a bike 'n hop on."

"I hear you," I said, chuckling as I lifted my hand in a goodbye salute and walked into the store.

I did hear him. But I knew I would never do that. Ed knew it too. That's why he lifted his hand holding the cigarette in a brief wave and shrugged slightly as he watched me disappear inside.

No doubt he had heard people say that before and nothing ever happened.

Driving the short three miles from Five Forks to our home in First Colony, I reflected on how that's the problem with so much of our living. We have a desire. We may even have a dream. But we are not quite ready to take the necessary steps required to reach our goal. We are not willing to "hop on the bike" that will take us to our desired destination.

Jesus said, "'I am the way and the truth and the life'" (John 14:6).

People say, "Oh, I would like to experience that. I would like to have the adventure of abundant life in the kingdom of God." But they count the cost and never hop on.

Ed's grunt and cynical smile were on target. So far, I haven't even priced a Harley-Davidson.

"Just call me Ed" was right. He was also right when he said the only way I could share his experiences was to grab the handlebars and jump on. It's the only way to reach California on a Harley.

Even more importantly, it's also the only way to reach Mullinix. Both rides can be breathtaking.

# A Groom's Beach Walk

Our little family group was lying on blankets or relaxing on beach chairs under two umbrellas on the beach in Kill Devil Hills, North Carolina. My wife, Jean, was quietly talking to one of our granddaughters, Sara, about her upcoming first year of college.

The conversation between Jean and Sara was becoming a distant murmur as I was being mesmerized by the rhythm of the white caps racing in to break in an explosion of gurgling water on the beach. Suddenly, my quiet reverie was interrupted by an exuberant voice shouting, "We just got married!"

I glanced up quickly to see a young couple strolling between us and the rising tide. The voice belonged to a smiling young man dressed in a black tuxedo, craning his neck around his bride to make eye contact with me.

"Pretty flowers!" my wife called out to the bride, who was gracefully holding her flowing white dress out of the sand with her right hand, which also held a large bouquet of wildflowers. Naturally, that was the first thing Jean noticed—being a former florist and avid lover of wildflowers.

The bride was stunning, but I could not take my eyes off the groom. "We just got married!" he shouted again when he realized we had locked eyes.

I briefly thought how that was an unrivaled example of stating the obvious—and I've preached a lot of sermons.

But as our eyes remained locked, I could easily imagine the rest of what he wanted to tell me: "I just can't believe this happened!" The young groom had an open, honest, likable face, but his physical attributes obviously belonged in the minor leagues compared to the major league beauty walking beside him.

Instantly recognizing that contrast, I readily understood the beaming face. *Beaming* does not do his visage justice, however. The groom was ecstatic—little rays of light shooting out in all directions—rivaling even the bright sun visible over his left shoulder. Clearly he did not think he deserved the great good fortune of this divine creature choosing to unite her life with his.

His smile grew even wider as he glanced in wonder at his bride and then back at me—as if wanting to leave no doubt in my mind that I was witnessing a true miracle.

"Can you believe it!" his facial expression exclaimed. "Out of all this beautiful woman's hundreds of choices, she chose *me*."

I kept smiling and nodding my head in congratulations to make certain he knew that I understood the wonder of it all. He returned my smiles and nods with unconstrained exuberance.

Before they moved too far down the beach, I gave him a congratulatory two thumbs up. The still smiling groom tried to reply with a thumbs up of his own, only to stumble on the loose sand. His bride gracefully reached down and pulled him upright.

"Poor fellow," I thought. "Can't even do two things at once. Can't walk and give me a thumbs up without falling on his face."

But I wasn't worried about the stumbles I knew were still to come for my friend at first sight. He was greatly blessed to have this lovely creature to walk beside him and keep him upright and lift him up when he fell. It was easy to understand the sublime ecstasy on his face. He was filled with overwhelming gratitude.

An unexpected wave of sadness suddenly swept over me, however, as the newlyweds passed on down the beach out of sight. It was as if a flash of hope had passed in front of my eyes for a few moments and just as quickly disappeared.

That happens too often in this world, it seems. Hope appears but then moves on much too quickly into the distant sunset.

But then as I lay back on my beach recliner, another realization crept in—I had seen that face before. I had seen that face as I lifted it out of the waters of baptism, dripping wet but with a light no amount of water could extinguish.

I had seen that face as it stepped out to give me a warm hug at the front of the sanctuary, accompanied by the whispered words, "I just heard God call my name, and I'm answering."

I had seen that face as death approached and her glowing face exclaimed, "Pastor, I'm going to see Jesus tonight!"

All along the way, in unexpected times and places, that face has kept appearing. And every once in a while, when I'm at my best, I see that face in the mirror as I recall that well-known but always amazing verse: "For God so loved the world that he gave his one and only Son, that whoever believes in him shall not perish but have eternal life" (John 3:16).

"God, how could you do it? How could you send your Son—your beautiful, precious, sinless Son—to die for me and walk beside me and lift me up when I stumble? How could you choose to unite your life with a bumbling creature like me, who can't seem to get out of his own way? That you would choose *me*—far above all my deserving!"

That groom's glowing face on the beach at Kill Devil Hills pops into my mind every once in a while. Each time it happens, I pray that somewhere along your journey, you too will catch a glimpse of that face. And that once in a while you will also be fortunate enough to see it in the mirror.

I must warn you, however: The image might leave you a little breathless.

# My Home Is the Ground

"I love the smell of old church buildings," my daughter Cheryl said. Smiling as we walked through the short hallway into the sanctuary of Saluda Baptist Church, I replied, "Yep. Has the smell of history and tradition and years of struggling to follow the Christ."

Cheryl and her family had come up from North Augusta, South Carolina, for my last Sunday after serving four years as interim pastor at this historic church. During my years there, we celebrated Saluda's 175th anniversary.

My daughter and I had just walked from the fellowship hall, which had been built much more recently and always had a clean, scrubbed aroma. The women who cared for the kitchen and the fellowship hall were serious about cleanliness, and the glistening surfaces reflected their meticulous care.

The contrast in feel and smell between the two areas of the church triggered a memory of a few months back. As I took my place on the bench beside the pulpit, listening to the prelude music, I found it hard to shake the memories our conversation had stirred.

It was a Wednesday night, and as usual I walked from my office through the kitchen into the fellowship hall to prepare for our prayer meeting. On this night, however, I immediately became aware that something was highly unusual.

A sour, acrid odor overwhelmed the customary aroma of cleansing molecules swirling around that space. The source of that dramatic change quickly became evident as a man dressed in several layers of dirty clothing walked toward me from where he had been sitting at a table near the double-door entrance.

Smiling, he reached out to shake my hand. The hand was rough and layered with several days of accumulated grime. I blinked my eyes rapidly to chase the tears that involuntarily filled them as a result of the potency of the stranger's unwashed body and clothing.

"Hi," I said. "I'm Jerry Haywood, the pastor."

Nodding, the man looked at me with surprisingly clear, intelligent eyes. But instead of telling me his name, he said, "Just stopping in to get out of the cold for a while." Looking at me warily, he continued, "If that's ok."

"Of course," I replied, pulling one of the metal chairs from the nearest table to sit opposite him. "Can I help you with anything?"

It was not unusual to have strangers stop by the church since we were located just down George Puller Highway from the Middlesex County courthouse and the main—or, perhaps I should say, *only*—intersection in the pleasant little village of

Saluda. But never had I seen anyone wander in who was so unkempt and caustically odiferous.

After we had talked for a while, during which time I learned his name was George, I asked him if he would like to join us around the table for forty-five minutes of Bible study and prayer. George quickly and enthusiastically said he would enjoy that.

The ten people who gathered on most Wednesday evenings welcomed George warmly, as I knew they would, even though it also took them several minutes to become acclimated to his potent aroma. George appeared disinterested through much of the study time, although he did occasionally contribute a random thought.

Following the prayer time, all of us—including those just arriving for choir practice—began asking George again what help we could offer. Bill Sigler, the former pastor of Saluda, who finally had to resign during a tough fight with cancer, reached into his wallet and said, "I've been wondering what I was supposed to do with this hundred-dollar bill," as he handed it to me.

I had always felt a kinship with Bill, who played football at my alma mater in Chapel Hill a few years after my graduation in 1963. But the real reason for our friendship was my admiration for the way he handled his illness with unequaled strength and deep faith. Bill showed us all what it meant to trust God's promise that his grace is sufficient for all our needs.

His spontaneous generosity also sparked an immediate reaching for wallets and pocketbooks by all those present. So with money in hand, I called a motel over in the tiny community of Topping and secured a room for George for the night.

As others wandered into choir practice or headed home, George held up an empty, faded blue pillowcase—a part of his luggage ensemble—and said, "I need a few supplies at Food Lion before we go—if you don't mind."

The local Food Lion was just down the road, so we circled by there before heading to Topping.

One of my stereotypes of the homeless population was quickly dispelled as I watched George carefully read the nutrition labels of every item he placed in his shopping cart. I had expected him to grab handfuls of junk food and sugary drinks. But the opposite occurred as he explained to me the health benefits of each item. I was surprised that he knew and cared much more about proper nutrition than I did.

Noting that I was somewhat mystified, George explained, "When you live on the ground like I do, you have to watch what you put into your body or you'll get sick for sure."

Earlier, I had made the mistake of calling George "homeless." He had protested vigorously, almost angrily, as he replied, "I'm not homeless! My home is the ground!" Back in the early 1990s George had simply made the decision that from that time forward, he would lay claim to the ground as his "home."

Maybe George had discovered something that many of us overlook. At its core the human journey, it seems to me, is a spiritual search for home—which more often than not ends in futility. We look to places and people and things and successes and accomplishments to fill that empty feeling of homelessness—of being orphaned in a lonely universe.

One of the most frightening things for parents is to lose the grip on a child's hand in a crowd and frantically wondering if we will find them. I remember being packed shoulder to shoulder along Duke of Gloucester Street in Williamsburg, Virginia, on July 4, 1976, when it seemed the whole world had come to celebrate the 200th anniversary of our country's Declaration of Independence.

One of my two youngest children, Chris, was on my back while the other, Brian, was in my arms. Jean held tightly to Cheryl's hand, our oldest, walking beside her. We knew that if they took even one step away from us, our children would be lost in that pressing mob.

But as a pastor for almost fifty years, I've also seen that happen to adults. Adults who suddenly lose their grip on that which they have called "home"—that which had given them a place to belong—and wonder if they will ever be found. Or if anyone is even looking for them.

After George had filled two of his faded blue pillowcases with assorted groceries, we piled back into my car and headed for the motel—which, we discovered on arriving, had closed. I remarked wryly, "George, I think you read one nutrition label too many."

He didn't think it was funny and wanted to knock on one of the occupied rooms to ask where we could find the management. I discouraged that idea quickly—much to his chagrin.

"I'm not stupid!" George shouted as I guided him back to the car.

"No," I replied. "You're certainly not stupid. You're a much smarter shopper than I am."

I chose not to add that when the occupant of a random motel room—most likely a burly long-distance trucker or construction worker—would answer the knock and stare out into the darkness at George in all his disheveled, odiferous splendor, we were both likely to be attacked or, at the very least, arrested. Thankfully, I was finally able to cool his anger and wounded pride sufficiently to get him back in the car and head back to Saluda.

Knowing the choir was still rehearsing, I called the church and was able to talk to one of our church leaders, Jennifer Lucas, who was also the church organist/pianist.

Jennifer informed me that she had a key to the parsonage, which was next door to the church, and thought it would be okay for George to spend the night there. I was deeply grateful because the next motel was in the next town and it was growing late. In addition, I still had an hour's drive back to my home in Williamsburg.

The option of simply leaving George outdoors on this bitterly cold night was something I didn't even contemplate. I was sure he had experienced many such nights on the ground, but I had not been able to do anything about that. Now, I felt I could make a difference.

As we pulled into the church parking lot, Jennifer met us with a key, and I helped George carry his bags of nutritional foods and drinks, along with his bedroll stuffed with all his belongings, into the parsonage.

Flipping on some lights, Jennifer led us into the bedroom and told George, "Clean sheets are already on the bed." We conversed casually for a few minutes before Jennifer turned to leave. George walked to the door to thank her.

When the two of us were alone, George looked around the bedroom apprehensively and asked hesitantly, "Do you mind if I put my bedroll on the floor in the living room and sleep there?"

"That's fine," I replied, looking at him questioningly.

"That bed looks a little high for me," he explained.

I guess I should have anticipated that. No doubt it did look high for someone who had spent at least half of his adult life sleeping on the ground.

After helping him get settled, I told him I thought I would head home. Immediately, George began talking feverishly, as someone starved for human interaction. He told me how his uncle had been a professor at UNC and he himself had taken a few courses before choosing to drop out and begin his nomadic existence.

Over the next hour, George enthralled me with hundreds of statistics gleaned from his vast knowledge of Carolina's athletic teams and laughed uproariously when I failed to answer questions he threw at me.

When he grew tired of my ignorance of sports trivia—even though I had always been fairly confident of my knowledge in that area—George moved on to some philosophers he had read and even a few theologians. Fortunately, I could answer more of those questions—mostly because they were essay type questions, which I've always been better at than multiple choice. At any rate, George seemed to be a little more pleased with me.

All of this confirmed one of my beliefs about the homeless. Many are very bright people but find it difficult to live in ordinary society, abiding by the norms established by the majority of us "normal" folk.

That clean, soft bed looked very appealing to me on this bitter night. But to George it was a menace. Two totally different ways of seeing the world.

I briefly wondered who was right and how many nights Jesus must have slept on the ground as he walked this earth—homeless, while inviting the world to find their home in him. After all, his birth in a feed trough was about as close to the ground as you can get without actually lying on the dirt.

An hour later, I was finally able to break away and head home, although my thoughts remained on the events of the past few hours. As I was leaving, George told me he planned to head up to the New England states as soon as the weather broke.

He seemed excited about it—a glint of hope lighting his eyes. I wish I had asked him what he expected to find there that he couldn't find in Virginia.

Staring through the thick darkness, searching to find my own way home over the black, narrow two-lane roads, the thought struck me that unlike most of us, George wasn't expecting to find "home"—a place to belong—in New England. He carried home with him. The ground, the whole earth, was his home—the one place where he felt he belonged.

A promise from Jesus suddenly pushed my other thoughts aside: "'Anyone who loves me will obey my teaching. My Father will love them, and we will come to them and make our home with them'" (John 14:23).

So maybe that's one of the secrets of "keeping on" in our journey to Mullinix—neither fearing homelessness nor settling for poor substitutes for home.

Our heavenly Parent has made his home within us.

# A 9/11 Wedding

The bride and groom were determined that the wedding was going to happen. They had been engaged for almost a year after dating for almost three. A lot of time and energy had gone into planning this big event.

Andy and Jill had graduated college in the same year, 1998, at schools miles apart. Andy graduated from Virginia Tech in Blacksburg, Virginia, while Jill earned her degree from Shepherd College in Shepherdstown, West Virginia, her hometown.

*Still Going to Mullinix*

Following graduation, both served internships at Ford's Colony in Williamsburg, Virginia, where Andy grew up. Coincidentally, however, they did not meet there, but met in June of 1998 while each was at a band concert with friends at The Jewish Mother, a popular restaurant in Williamsburg. Unfortunately, the restaurant burned to the ground the next year, but Andy and Jill's relationship thrived. They were engaged in December 2000.

Now, everything was in place. The dresses had been bought, the tuxedoes rented, and the caterers paid. The rehearsal was about to start.

But it was hard. It was emotional to the point of bringing tears. Some family members weren't even sure they should go ahead.

It was September 15, 2001. All the headlines were screaming "Evil Acts!" The nation and the world were in mourning, growing angrier by the day.

In addition, the wedding was being held in Shepherdstown, approximately seventy miles from the Pentagon, which had been one of the targets of the terrorists who destroyed the World Trade Center, killing over 2,000 people.

Shepherdstown was a wonderful venue for a wedding, with its quaint, old-world charm, resting along the banks of the Potomac River. Most consider this the oldest town in West Virginia—although people like to argue about such stuff.

To top off a perfect setting, Jill's parents had arranged for the bride and groom to climb into a white horse-drawn carriage and ride from the wedding to the reception. Every detail was carefully planned for a perfect wedding.

Then came the terrorist attacks, casting a shadow over all the festivities. Would this tragedy make it impossible for the wedding to be a true celebration? Would it even be appropriate to be happy when so many were feeling total despair? Would some friends and family be unable to make it to Shepherdstown because of travel restrictions?

Questions like these had caused the young couple sitting before me to wonder how all this was going to affect the happy occasion. It certainly didn't appear to be an ideal time for a wedding.

But in a broken world, is there ever an ideal time for *anything*? I read somewhere that C. S. Lewis said something to the effect that we are all "living on a precipice." For me, that speaks to the human condition of continuous vulnerability in the presence of crisis and despair and catastrophe. The next step could mean a plunge down the precipice.

But Andy and Jill dared take the next step. The wedding proceeded.

In my wedding meditation I acknowledged the fact that we live in a world where the sudden appearance of evil and its terrible consequences are always a threat. But in the midst of all that, we continue to have weddings because we have something stronger than the evil that threatens us.

So I characterized their wedding as an "island of hope" in the shadow of a "tower of terror."

The Apostle Paul seemed to recognize that most of our lives are lived under such threatening shadows when he reminded those Corinthians, "We have this treasure in jars of clay" (2 Cor 4:7). Clay jars can be easily broken. But that's not where the power lies. So Paul continues: "This all-surpassing power is from God and not from us. [*So because of that*] we are hard pressed on every side, but not crushed; perplexed, but not in despair; persecuted, but not abandoned; struck down, but not destroyed" (2 Cor 4:7–9, italics mine).

Evil does not have the final word.

During my retirement from the full-time pastorate, I have almost stopped performing weddings. The preparation and officiating of weddings take much more time and energy from the minister than most people imagine. These days, I choose to use most of my energy in writing and hiking and fishing.

Every once in a while, however, I remember that wedding in Shepherdstown, West Virginia—it has become for me a symbol of hope in the shadow of great pain and suffering. And I look at what that event has produced almost twenty years later.

Andy and Jill Lutz now live in Richmond, Virginia, with their two daughters, Claire, who enjoys playing soccer, and Charlotte, who is involved in dance and field hockey.

Jill is still teaching school and has become a fifth-grade teacher after guiding the minds and lives of first- and second-graders for almost twenty years. Andy worked in the golfing industry as a territory manager for many years and is now an estimator for a commercial construction company.

In the shadow of one of the greatest tragedies in our nation's history, Andy and Jill found an island of hope, and hope has not disappointed them (Rom 5:5).

By the way, everyone who was expected to attend made it to the wedding. We all felt comforted by being together.

So every once in a while, I will say "yes" to a couple asking if I will perform their marriage because I still believe that God's power is far greater than all the evil this world can hurl at us. Evil can harm and damage but not destroy.

The journey to Mullinix, the pilgrimage to authentic discipleship, is always a journey in the shadow of evil, I guess.

But here's the part that takes my breath away: Right there in the darkness is where hope lives and calls us onward.

# Did I Smile?

We were saying our goodbyes when Dorothy looked up at me with soft brown eyes and asked plaintively, "Did I smile?"

Four of the ladies in our church had asked me if I would like to drive over to Matthews, Virginia, to visit Dorothy. She had been in a nursing home for a couple years and was always happy to see folks from her home church.

Dorothy's mind was not as sharp as it once was, but she immediately recognized me as her pastor and asked me to sit beside her in the social hall where we had gathered. "I want to talk to you about my funeral," she said.

Unfortunately, when I settled in next to Dorothy, she could not remember what she had planned to tell me. I patted her on the shoulder and assured her it would come to her later as we moved on to other topics.

Time passed quickly as we all laughed and talked and told stories until noon when the women began setting out the baskets of food they had brought. A group of Baptist women know how to fill a buffet table. We also knew how to devour that feast.

Following the meal, Lucille Johnston gathered us around the piano in the social hall for a final picture. We placed Dorothy in the center. Immediately, everyone began encouraging her to smile. Throughout our visit, Dorothy had been very solemn. It looked as if her face had not been visited by a smile in a long time.

So a chorus of voices rang out as cameras started clicking: "Smile, Dorothy. Smile now." Dorothy kept trying to lift the corners of her tight mouth—never certain that she was being successful. After a few attempts, she grabbed the front of my shirt, pulled me down to where she sat in her wheelchair, and whispered, "Did I smile, Pastor? Did I smile?"

Bending closer to her ear, I whispered back, "You did good, honey. You did real good."

Truthfully, Dorothy's smile was just a hint of the real thing, but her face did look more pleasant, and her eyes brightened slightly. It was obvious she was making a valiant effort to smile.

We should all try so hard.

Smiles are a powerful form of communication. My younger son, Brian—especially in his early years—would often grow frustrated and angry and say, "I don't like him!" When I asked why, Brian would reply, "He never smiles." Smiles are powerful communicators of warmth, friendliness, and openness. Without them, it's difficult to know where we stand with the blank face in front of us.

So I was relieved when I recently renewed my driver's license and they told me I could smile. In December 2015, policy was changed to allow smiling faces on driver's licenses for the first time in six years in the state of Virginia. Smiling was originally prohibited—according to the DMV—because of the limitations of photo recognition technology. Thankfully, that technology has now advanced to the point where drivers have the option of grinning broadly from their licenses at the state trooper who pulls them over for speeding.

I also discovered, after the new policy was adopted in 2015, that Virginia residents could pay twenty dollars to have a new smiling visage placed on their existing license prior to the renewal date. I thought that was a reasonable price. In my opinion, smiles are worth far more than twenty dollars.

My father had the habit of humming with a pleasant look on his face as he approached people—especially strangers.

I asked him about that one time, and he said, "Humming helps me relax." Then he told how he and his siblings grew up in the woods above Little River in a kind of isolated environment. In a rare moment of self-revelation, he said, chuckling, "We were as shy and skittish as rabbits in those days. I guess I still have a little of that shyness."

For a time, while he was quite successful in the insurance business, meeting complete strangers was not the easiest thing for Daddy. Quiet humming helped.

I never did any humming, but I have always tried to present a smile to those I meet—not a wide, exaggerated, toothy smile—but a friendly smile to let them know I was open to pleasant interaction.

I have always trusted body language more than words—which has made things difficult for me at times.

While I was a pastor, meetings with more than three or four people around the table were complicated. My intense awareness of body language meant I was receiving simultaneous messages from all those gathered around the table. Trying to read the shifting postures and changing eye and facial expressions was always a challenge and sometimes overwhelming.

Consequently, I have always preferred one-on-one conversations and have tried never to discuss potentially controversial subjects over the phone. In my world, body language is essential for clear understanding. Today's text messages are minefields for misunderstandings.

I was counseling a married couple when the wife became extremely agitated at her spouse.

"What? What? I didn't say a word!" the husband exclaimed in exasperation.

"But you should see your face!" the wife fired back with a facial expression of her own much scarier than her words.

There is body language that is so dramatic that it's hard to miss or misunderstand. But there are much more subtle uses of the body that do require that we really "listen with our eyes" or body language can become the source of many of our misunderstandings of each other. Sometimes our listening and observing are so infected with prior negative feelings toward the person that body language—as important as it is—is misinterpreted.

"Pastor, did I smile?" I know, Dorothy. Sometimes it's hard to smile. And when we try, we're not even sure we pulled it off.

But here's the hopeful part. God has access to more of our body to "read" than our fellow pilgrims on the way to Mullinix. We're stuck with the external language of the body. God reads the inner parts, especially the heart: "We speak as those approved by God to be entrusted with the gospel. We are not trying to please people but God, who tests our hearts" (1 Thess 2:4).

It really is breathtaking to realize that God never misinterprets our heart language no matter how many wrong signals our body gives to others.

# Friendship Cake

It was a wedding much like all the others I had conducted over the past several decades—with one exception. Other than the bride and groom, I did not know anyone.

The groom, recently graduated from the College of W&M, had attended our church regularly during his undergraduate years. His family, in addition to the bride and her family, were all from out of town.

I have never been gifted at small talk with people with whom I share no history. I found it more comfortable, at the intimate house reception following the ceremony, to fill my plate with finger food, along with assorted nuts and mints, and sit alone at a corner table.

The solitude didn't last long. Just as I was settling in, the little blonde flower girl, a little older than most flower girls, came walking briskly over with her plate and small plastic cup of lemonade and plopped down beside me.

"Can I sit with you?" she asked cheerfully, even though she was already sliding into the chair next to me.

"Of course," I replied enthusiastically and honestly. Small talk with children is always interesting and fun.

We talked and laughed quietly while trying to identify some of the mysterious morsels of food on her plate. I was enjoying our conversation so much that when I glanced at my watch, I was surprised to see how fast the time had passed and stood up abruptly, reluctantly telling my new friend I had to go.

Startled, Emily jumped up, protesting with unexpected fervor, "No, no, no!" she cried. "You can't leave now!"

"I don't want to go, honey," I replied. "But I have to meet someone at church. They won't be happy if I don't show up."

"But we haven't cut the cake yet!" Emily cried emphatically. It was obvious that, to her, the cake-cutting was the most important part of the entire proceedings and she did not want me to miss such a momentous event.

"I know," I said soothingly. "I'm terribly disappointed too." Then, leaning over, I spoke in a conspiratorial whisper, "Someone told me the smaller groom's cake is a devil's food cake underneath all that white icing. I do hate to miss that." Then, pausing thoughtfully, I said, "We're friends, right?" She nodded her head rapidly. "So since we're such good friends, would you be willing to eat a piece of that cake for me? Think you can do that?"

Her big blue eyes widened as she nodded even more energetically. Emily followed closely on my heels as I went over to tell the bride and groom goodbye. She then stood at the door, watching me walk down the front steps. I was almost at the end of the long, curving concrete walk when I heard her cry out as she came running toward me.

I immediately stopped and turned, wondering what she had forgotten to tell me. Tilting her pretty head to one side, she said, "I was just thinking. If I eat the first piece of cake for *you*, I'll have to eat *two* pieces, or I won't get any."

"I never thought of that," I said, laughing. "But you're right. You *have* to eat two pieces, or you won't get any cake at all." Satisfied, Emily turned and skipped happily back up the walk.

Driving to my church study, chuckling softly at Emily's words, I suddenly realized the profundity of what had just happened. "Maybe my little friend understood real friendship in that moment more than most of us do in a lifetime," I muttered to myself.

Emily identified with me and my needs so intimately that eating that first piece of cake was all about me and had nothing to do with her own desires. The fact that she was, in reality, going to get two pieces of cake never entered her mind. Her focus was on being willing to forego her enjoyment to make sure I had my share of cake.

That's when it occurred to me that Emily had just demonstrated a major building block for real friendship—empathy.

As a friend, Jesus says that he is willing to open his whole mind to the other: "'I no longer call you servants, because a servant does not know his master's business. Instead, I have called you friends, for everything that I learned from my Father I have made known to you'" (John 15:15).

As a friend, Jesus says he listens, and he answers. To me, that is another way of saying that he feels with us—just as on that day he wept with Mary and Martha over the death of Lazarus. Surely Jesus knew he was going to restore life to Lazarus. But he was so moved by the grief of his close friends that he wept along with them.

In my mind, that's a pretty good definition of empathy. It's also a pretty good demonstration of being church.

I remember the woman who looked at me with painful eyes, red and swollen from hours of crying over the death of one she loved deeply, and said, "Pastor, how do people go on without a church?" She felt she could make it if she just had friends with enough empathy to feel with her and cry with her.

I often think of little Emily and wonder how many others were blessed in how many ways through her offer to eat that first piece of cake for them.

Such friendship makes it possible for all of us to take a deep breath and continue our journey toward achieving authentic discipleship.

# Part Seven

A Breathtaking Journey

Is Filled with Insights

# Mixed Motives

"Pastor Jerry, I think fifty percent I want to be baptized for the right reason and fifty percent because you're leaving. So I'm going to wait."

Catherine Spratt had been a participant in my pastor's class some months back. As we talked about the basic tenets of the Christian faith, it became evident that Catherine was one of the brightest and most conscientious members of this class.

I always made it clear to the children that completion of the pastor's class was not an automatic step into the baptistery and church membership. They should be sure that God was calling them to that next stage of their discipleship.

But another dynamic had now entered into Catherine's decision. I had announced my retirement, which would take place six months later. After serving as pastor at Walnut Hills for thirty-five years, I was, of course, the only pastor most of the young people had known.

So a parade of people made their way to my study to talk about making commitments and being baptized before I left—decisions many of them had been delaying for no good reason. In a recent meeting, the chairman of the baptismal committee at the time, Doug Brown, said, "Every time I turned around, we were filling the baptistery."

I became a little concerned. Were they doing this for the right reason or because I was leaving? Oh, I was thoroughly enjoying all these baptisms. The Hampton Roads sewer and water billing service called and said they thought we had a water leak at the church.

"No," I replied cheerfully. "We're baptizing."

"Wha—?" the voice on the other end of the line started to ask when I interrupted to explain.

"We're Baptists."

Now it was time for the friendly woman to interrupt. "I understand," she said. "I grew up in a little Baptist church out in the country. Baptists use a lot of water. But we were mostly baptized in the river." She paused briefly before continuing, "The Rappahannock over in Middlesex County, especially around Deltaville, has some nice sandy places."

"We had some river baptisms when I was growing up in North Carolina," I said. "But it's a little hard to find a warm spot on the James during the winter." She laughed and hung up. I hoped maybe our immediate friendship would entitle our church to a little discount on the next water bill. It didn't happen.

During one Sunday morning service, I expressed my desire that the baptismal decisions not be based solely on the fact that I was leaving. That's when Catherine came to my study and said she was struggling. She made the mature decision, for a nine-year-old, to wait.

But a couple months later, Catherine walked down the aisle at the conclusion of worship and whispered in my ear, "Pastor Jerry, I'm ninety-eight percent sure I'm doing this for the right reason."

I whispered back to her, "Honey, ninety-eight percent is much higher than the percentage of certainty I usually reach before acting. Let's do it."

Waiting for the proper motivation to act is an admirable thing. But I have sometimes been in the position of being too careful and waiting too long. Truth be told, I have sometimes waited so long in an attempt to fully understand God's will that I never acted at all.

I remember a meeting held at our church sometime in the 1970s. A variety of community leaders had come together on a Thursday morning to address the housing needs of seasonal workers at Colonial Williamsburg. That was a big issue in the community at the time.

Ideas flew around the room until it finally became obvious that no clear direction was emerging. We were terribly frustrated. So many ideas were tossed into the air that we could grab hold of none of them.

Finally, a burly contractor who was a well-respected builder in the community stood up and said, "Folks, looks like we're trying to find the perfect solution, and none of us knows what that is." He cleared his throat before continuing, "That's not surprising because most of the time there is no *perfect* answer. When I reach those places in my business decisions, I just go ahead and act on my *best* knowledge. Otherwise, nothing ever gets done." The meeting became much more productive after that.

Just so, with ninety-eight percent certainty, Catherine acted, and I had the joy of baptizing her prior to my retirement.

Discerning God's will is not easy, despite what those folks who claim to think God's thoughts after him and sometimes *before* him would have us believe.

Even such a spiritual giant as the Apostle Paul had problems understanding God's will at times. He even struggled over those things about which he should pray: "In the same way, the Spirit helps us in our weakness. We do not know what we ought to pray for, but the Spirit himself intercedes for us through wordless groans" (Rom 8:26).

We need to be conscientious and do all we can to discern God's will. But we must guard against being *too* careful. So careful that we fail to act at all. There are times along the journey to Mullinix when we must hold our breath and, by faith, take the next uncertain step.

Catherine Spratt is now a nurse in the coronary care unit at Saint Mary's Hospital in Richmond. I have instructed my wife that if I ever have a critical coronary event, I want Catherine to take care of me.

I trust her decisions, especially in matters of the heart.

# Sophisticated School Lunches

During my almost fifty years as a pastor, I have spent a large portion of that time in hospitals with parishioners and relatives of parishioners. Those hours and days and weeks and months would certainly add up to years.

I never resented any of those times because I learned very early in my ministry that unless you are present for the crises of life, people do not trust you as a pastor and friend. Since, as the saying goes, "the only minor surgery is that performed on someone else," I tried to be there for those undergoing even the smallest of procedures. Lasting relationships were forged during those hospital hours.

I also discovered that those times were filled with valuable, heartfelt sharing. We tend to bare our souls more easily during a time of anxiety and crisis.

I have fond memories of all those people, but I want to tell you of just one whom I came to know much better during a morning of awaiting the completion of her mother's lengthy surgery. On this particular day, most of our waiting took place in the hospital cafeteria—which was not unusual. Sitting around a table was more relaxing for most families than camping out in the surgical waiting room.

We were not being very successful at enjoying the bland hospital breakfast, so we began reminiscing about the food of our growing up years. My friend was recalling how her mother would pack her school lunches in a galvanized pail bucket. This was long before those fancy lunch boxes with Cinderella and all the superheroes like Batman and Superman came out.

"How I hated that lunch pail!" she said with the intensity of memories that still stung. "I knew that lunch pail screamed *country* to all my classmates." She chuckled and added, "Of course, that was long before everyone thought moving to the country was a sign of success and sophistication."

We were quiet for a few moments as we struggled to wash down crumbly, day-old hospital biscuits with lukewarm coffee. Studying one of those biscuits without actually seeing it, she continued, "I ate a lot of lunches alone during those years. Not because I didn't have friends, but because I was embarrassed about the homemade biscuits Mother had made that morning before school and filled with country ham cured in my daddy's smokehouse."

I looked down at my cold scrambled eggs and limp bacon with deep sadness. "Usually, Mother had also packed a baked sweet potato left over from the night before." Now my companion was forcing a rueful smile. "How I envied my classmates from town who were bringing sandwiches made out of sliced white bread and bologna. During those years, sliced white bread was a sure sign of class." Her memories were spilling over each other now. "Sometimes they even had Nabs! I had never in my life had store-bought, sliced-white-bread bologna sandwiches with Nabs on the side."

I was momentarily lost in my own memories—not of lunch pails, because we used brown paper bags for our banana sandwiches liberally slathered with Duke's mayonnaise. All schools seem to have a distinctive aroma. Mt. Gilead Elementary School smelled like a giant banana sandwich during my student days.

My memories were suddenly interrupted as my friend continued, "So you can imagine my surprise on the day one of my classmates walked over to the table where I sat alone and asked if I would trade lunches with her." This time her laughter was genuine in its self-deprecation. "Naturally, I didn't hesitate and sat there and ate that bland, sliced-white-bread and cold bologna sandwich with sophisticated pride. Finally, I had arrived. So every day I was happy to exchange lunches with her."

My companion's description of her country ham biscuit and baked sweet potato lunches had made it impossible for me to eat any more of the hospital breakfast, so I pushed it aside and waited for her to finish her story.

Her eyes were wet now with unshed tears, and I knew her memories of years past had become mingled with anxiety over her mother's present-day surgery. "Can you believe I did that?" she asked suddenly. "I spent all those years trading homemade biscuits filled with smokehouse-cured ham for white-bread bologna sandwiches and Nabs." Chuckling softly, she said, "And the bologna wasn't even fried."

She paused thoughtfully before concluding, "Isn't it funny how we do that? I mean trade the best for the less. I would give anything to have Mother pack that galvanized lunch pail for me just one more time."

Thinking the surgery should be about over, we rode the elevator to the surgical area and waited for the doctor. Each of us became lost in our own memories in the quiet room. My thoughts now centered on the sermon for the next Sunday my friend had just given me—constantly deceiving ourselves about the right food to satisfy our hunger.

I thought of the Scripture passage I might use for that sermon. Jesus said, "'Do not work for food that spoils, but for food that endures to eternal life, which the Son of Man will give you.... I am the bread of life. Whoever comes to me will never go hungry'" (John 6:27, 35).

Jesus was as clear as he could have been. Still, we keep tasting all kinds of "bread" in a mad scramble to get what we believe will fill our emptiness and satisfy our starved lives. Then, when all the grabbing is over, we despair to learn that we have settled for food that promised much but delivered little.

As we silently awaited the surgeon, I renewed my prayer that on the way to Mullinix, I would be able to discern the difference between authentic country ham biscuits and bland, sliced-white-bread substitutes masquerading as the "best."

*Still Going to Mullinix*

We also bowed our heads and whispered a prayer of thanksgiving a few minutes later when the doctor told us my friend's mother would be all right.

Relaxing and sighing deeply, my friend smiled and said, "I didn't realize I had been holding my breath."

I gave her a quick hug and replied, "Life can have many kinds of breathtaking experiences. I'm glad this was one of the happy ones."

# The Tonsillectomy

"Daddy, how do they take it out?" My eight-year-old son, Chris, and I were walking hand in hand down a Williamsburg Community Hospital hallway. All kinds of illnesses had been springing up from diseased tonsils, so we were here to have it taken care of by a local general surgeon, Dr. George Oliver.

Chris's trust in me was complete as I explained the necessity of the operation. In fact, as he showed off his new light blue bathrobe to the nurses, Chris was enjoying being the center of attention.

But this sudden question startled me: How do you tell a trusting eight-year-old that taking out his tonsils involved cutting on the inside of his throat? We had been inseparable since his birth, and he felt I could do no wrong and was invincible.

On one of those extremely rare occasions when I was bedridden for a couple days with the flu, Chris became very anxious and silent—neither of which was his normal approach to life. He was always happy, loud, and in constant motion.

So his silence was troubling until he whispered quietly to his mother as they slipped away from the bedroom door where they had come to check on me: "Mama, I didn't know Daddy could get sick."

I was invincible in his eyes and totally trustworthy. Now I was letting them wheel Chris out of my sight to be cut on by strangers. I felt miserable that I was somehow betraying his trust by not telling him the truth. On the other hand, I worried about replacing his exuberant confidence with abject fear.

Like we do as fathers sometimes, I gave a vague answer and tried to turn his attention in another direction.

My heart was breaking, and I felt a piece of me was also being surgically removed as I helped him onto the gurney and walked beside him to the double doors, where I was told this was as far as I could go. My chest tightened as I imagined his response to the bright lights of the operating room and strange eyes looking down at him above frightening masks. (This, of course, was long before everyone wore masks in response to the coronavirus pandemic of 2020.)

Even though I knew this surgery was necessary and best for him in the long run, I felt I had terribly betrayed a little boy's trust in his father. Rational thought is not always capable of overcoming irrational feelings.

I still have vivid memories of the dingy beige carpeting in the hospital waiting room and the worn trail I created as I compulsively paced back and forth while jabbering incoherently. My wife looked up from her magazine and said, "Why don't you sit down. It won't be long. You're getting on my nerves."

*Still Going to Mullinix*

"Can't help it," I replied irritably, slightly angry that my fragile hold on sanity was being strained even farther. Friends who had come to keep us company kept trying to distract me with conversations on a variety of topics, but these were only unwelcome intrusions into my single-minded focus on what was happening to Chris in the operating room.

Reflecting on that experience later, I began to see that this must have been something of what Paul meant when he said: "Brothers and sisters, I do not consider myself yet to have taken hold of it. But one thing I do: Forgetting what is behind and straining toward what is ahead, I press on toward the goal to win the prize for which God has called me heavenward in Christ Jesus" (Phil 3:13–14).

Single-minded focus is necessary if we are to become authentic disciples. Nothing should be allowed to compromise my attention as I make my way toward Christlikeness.

Now, focus has never been a problem for me. One morning, I was struggling to put the finishing touches on a sermon when a stranger walked in.

"Hi," he said cheerfully, extending his hand. "I'm James Beckett."

Looking up with glazed eyes, I stammered, "I'm..."

I hesitated just long enough for the man to say with a laugh, "I was told you're Jerry Haywood."

"You're absolutely correct," I replied with an apologetic laugh.

Later, after overhearing that conversation, my secretary asked with a smile, "Am I going to have to start introducing you to everyone who comes in?"

"Actually," I said, trying to smile, "I would much prefer that you stop anyone from coming in when I'm concentrating on the final draft of my sermon. I'm not responsible for anything I say at that time."

And that's the way Linda Leffler and I did it for over twenty years.

So, like I said, I have never had a problem with single-minded focus. Paul's words in his letter to the Philippians have never been difficult for me to understand or appreciate.

The surgery turned out fine—as everyone but I had expected—although it took Chris much longer to recover than his sister, Cheryl, who had the same surgery at age five. Our biggest challenge with Cheryl was keeping her from going out and playing as soon as we returned home from the hospital. She even asked for popcorn on the day following surgery.

Chris's recovery, on the other hand, took so long that we returned to Dr. Oliver, who assured us that the operation looked fine and Chris had probably contracted a nasty bug that was currently making its way through the schools.

I stayed with Chris during that first long night in the hospital. He was so uncomfortable that he moaned almost continuously as I held him in my lap.

A nurse became so irritated that she came in and angrily told Chris to be quiet or she was going to make me leave. "That's not going to happen," I said emphatically. "Besides, no one can hear him outside this room." Sensing my determination and anger, she left hurriedly with no suggestion for relieving his discomfort.

A couple minutes later, the very kind head nurse—who no doubt had overheard our conversation, which was much louder than Chris's moaning—came in to offer assistance and words of comfort.

I asked if she would give me the name of the nurse I had dismissed. She kept deflecting my question and never revealed her name. But I found it telling that in all my subsequent years of visiting parishioners in Williamsburg Community Hospital, I never saw that nurse. I hoped I had not contributed to her being fired. Maybe something awful had happened to her that day, or perhaps she also was ill. I even thought about inquiring about her, but I never knew her name. I felt bad about that.

But I never felt bad that on the night of my eight-year-old son's surgery, my focus was completely on him. And so even though I later had regrets about the consequences the rude and unsympathetic nurse may have experienced, I had no regrets about my single-minded attention to Chris's needs. That was the most important thing at the time, and focus made it possible for me to give him the best care possible.

That seems to also work in this business of becoming a true disciple. "This one thing I do" describes Paul's single-minded "pressing on" focus in his breathtaking journey toward "the heavenly call of God in Christ Jesus."

*Still Going to Mullinix*

# The Sound of Silence

Energetic steps accompanied by the leather heels of dress shoes tap dancing down the empty hallways echoed throughout the silent church.

This was back before the sad time when we felt it was necessary to lock church buildings. So I had remained at my desk and allowed my guest to enter through the always unlocked and welcoming front doors.

Everyone had left for the day. To say it was quiet would not do justice to the silence; it was so thick that it was almost visible to the naked eye. The clicking heels suddenly stopped as the handsome, athletic young man strolled confidently into my carpeted study.

Earlier that week, he had made an appointment to discuss insurance. I didn't usually make appointments with salesmen of any kind—especially following a tiring day of work. But I had watched this young man play basketball for the College of William & Mary just a few years earlier, and being a sports enthusiast, I have always enjoyed talking to athletes.

We began with small talk, which has never been my favorite form of conversation. But as we talked, I noticed that the young man also became increasingly uncomfortable—squirming in the well-padded chair at the corner of my desk, looking around furtively. I wondered briefly if he disliked small talk as much as I did.

My question was answered immediately, however, when he blurted out, "How can you stand this *quiet?*" So that was his problem. Too much silence. I tried not to judge him too harshly since he had grown up with screaming fans almost within arm's reach, accompanying his every move.

I knew that scene well since I had always dropped off my high school basketball team—even the year the coach had unexpectedly (and probably undeservedly) named me starting point guard. The deafening noise in that tiny gym was too disturbing. I had no problem with the noise throughout the baseball and football seasons because there was a space buffer between me and the spectators.

But the screaming, claustrophobic environment of a small high school gymnasium was too much for my sensibilities. Thankfully, my younger brother, Kent, a sharpshooting guard, carried on the Haywood name throughout the basketball season while I peacefully absorbed the quiet of the woods as I sat with my back against the thick trunk of a large pine tree.

Most often, my empty 12-gauge shotgun was propped against the same tree as I thrilled at our family's four beagles chasing a rabbit in widening circles around me. It was just as enjoyable to trudge through thick fields where those same beagles jumped a rabbit and took off to the races while I looked for the nearest tree with a soft bed of pine needles at its base.

No one understood. Even our principal, I. B. Shive, called me in and asked if I had a problem with the basketball coach—who was actually a good friend.

When I told him it was the noise I could not tolerate, he merely shook his head in puzzlement and dropped it. He had watched me perform at shortstop in baseball and at halfback and safety in football since I was a freshman. Even in our small town, both of those sports drew a sizable number of spectators. Mr. Shive could not understand the difference.

School counselors qualified to explain such strange behavioral quirks had not yet been invented. Or at least they had not yet arrived in Mt. Gilead.

My long-ago memories were suddenly interrupted as my restless guest began noisily shuffling papers, obviously eager to get on with his sales pitch and leave. "So silence bothers you?" I asked, suddenly realizing my words sounded like the beginning of a counseling session, which neither he nor I was up to at the moment.

"I just can't think with all this quiet," he replied with an apologetic shake of his head. "Well," I said smiling, "we could make another appointment for earlier in the day tomorrow. I feel certain that I could persuade a few of the preschoolers from our Learning Center to come over and run relays in the hallway while we talk."

Laughing and relaxing slightly, he said, "Thanks, but I think maybe I can plow through it." He did, but it was obvious that he cut his prepared speech short so he could rush out and rejoin his much more comfortable noisy world.

Reflecting on that experience later, I wondered if our different approach to silence was mostly a generational phenomenon. There is no doubt that all the modern electronic devices—most small enough to carry on our person at all times—place noise, pumped up as loud as we desire, at our constant disposal. I have seen members of the younger generation desperately lunge for their noise-making devices as soon as there was an unexpected moment of silence.

On the other hand, television didn't come to my hometown until I was twelve years old. Also, our little Philco radio was so staticky that we mostly left it off except tor the Yankees baseball games—even though the hot August days made it even more staticky than usual. The play-by-play by Mel Allen would often be indiscernible, so we would hear the fans roaring with no idea what had just happened.

Silence was often preferable to the frustration. My generation grew up in an entirely different environment than today's youth.

But I wondered if our differing attitude toward silence was more complex than a generational divide. Perhaps it also had an element of the experiential. What had been our individual experience with silence?

Silence for this young athlete probably meant that his team was losing. Or, at the very least, nothing exciting was happening. Did silence mean failure for him?

On the other hand, most of my experiences with silence had to do with family. I remember early summer evenings when we would gather under the huge oak tree at the edge of our backyard.

The sun was slowly setting behind Joe Haywood's house on the hill just beyond his cow pasture. The growing twilight ushered in a palpable silence as we burst open a well-ripened watermelon harvested from the field next to the barn—fifty yards down a slight incline from where we had gathered.

The watermelon was delicious even though it was still warm from lying in the sun all day. Still, the taste of the watermelon and the sight of the seeds rocketing from our spitting mouths through the growing twilight are not my primary memories of those quiet summer evenings.

Foremost is the memory of family. Of course, I can't forget the lonely cry of the whippoorwill from down the hill and just across the creek. However, the "lonely" never quite touched us. We were family. We knew we were loved, and that love was a warm blanket shielding us from the cold world.

Experiencing family was what that silence was all about for me.

Later that evening, just before bedtime, we would gather in our small living room, where Daddy would read from the Bible and pray. I don't remember any of the Bible verses or any of his prayers, but I distinctly remember the tone of his voice. It had no similarity to the "ministerial tone" so often associated with the superficiality and forced professionalism we sometimes encounter.

Rather, his voice took on such a degree of gravity that I knew reading the Bible and praying were not to be approached casually or carelessly but were to be revered. My father's tone was like a verbal sign flashing the message—"Sacred: Tread Softly."

When my own children were young, I tried to duplicate this experience at the dinner table. But noise was always coming from somewhere—most notably from neighborhood children begging for our three children, Cheryl, Chris, and Brian, to come out and play.

So instead of possessing the quiet tones of my father's voice, I heard myself becoming loud and almost harsh as I demanded quiet. I was especially aware of this the day our daughter Cheryl looked at me in total exasperation and said, "Daddy, you like peace too much!"

Maybe I do. And no doubt individual personality also enters into this whole business of an appreciation for silence. As an introvert I function better in silence. It gives me the opportunity to retreat inside and work things out in a place of calm.

I acknowledge that more extroverted folks can find strength in meeting God right in the middle of all life's noises. I have no doubt he is with us in all noisy places.

But as I make my way toward Mullinix—that place where a more authentic discipleship becomes an established lifestyle—I can't help but wonder if we are missing something significant if we fail to find those places where we follow the command to "be still, and know that I am God" (Ps 46:10).

Following the great contest between Elijah and the prophets of Baal on Mt. Carmel, an exhausted and depressed Elijah runs into the wilderness, begging God to let him die. But God has other plans and calls Elijah out of the cave to stand on the mountaintop. Elijah obeys and waits for God to show up.

When Elijah had been demonstrating the power of his God, there was wind and earthquake and fire. Oh, Elijah looked like a magician with all kinds of heavenly fireworks at his disposal. It was as loud and exciting as any Fourth of July celebration Colonial Williamsburg has ever put on for the thousands of visitors who come to watch on that holiday.

God was present and at work in all that riotous noise. But the inner experience of communicating with God—*knowing* God—came through a "still small voice" (1 Kgs 19:12b, KJV).

The phrase "still small voice" is difficult to translate. The New Revised Standard Version reads, "a sound of sheer silence." The New International Version translates the phrase as "a gentle whisper." The New Jerusalem version reads "the sound of a gentle breeze," while the New English Bible translates it as "a low, murmuring sound."

But all these translations seem to be clear on one fact: Hearing God—really getting to *know* God—requires quiet listening. To bring meaning into all the noisy times, to hear God's word of guidance as to where we should go and what we should do and who we should be, to find God's purpose in our lives, we need times and places of silence and solitude.

Only when the fireworks had ended did Elijah really hear something. And what he heard took his breath away.

# My Own Worst Enemy

It was the middle of the night, and I had been in a deep sleep for several hours. But that didn't keep my adrenalin level from suddenly leaping heavenward as my body tensed—ready for battle.

My wife and I were staying at a hotel in Winston-Salem, where I was to officiate at my niece Jackie's wedding the next day. As happens more often these days, I was making my customary trip to a middle of the night call of nature.

Cautiously feeling my way in the darkness toward where I remembered the bathroom to be, I saw what I assumed was the doorway on my right. But as I began stepping through it, my progress was abruptly halted as I bumped noses with a stranger.

It's remarkable how quickly you can arouse from a sound sleep and assume the fighting posture. My eyes widened, and my tightened fists flew up in a protective boxer's stance.

The fight never materialized, however, as I suddenly looked into the eyes of not a stranger but a very familiar face. The "doorway" turned out to be a full-length mirror on the wall next to the bathroom door. I had bumped noses with myself.

After regaining my composure, I burst into uncontrollable laughter, which I tried to muffle so as not to awaken my wife. I must have been only partially successful because the next morning Jean asked me, "Did I hear you laughing during the night?"

"Yeah," I replied, chuckling. "Got into a little skirmish with myself."

Of course, that wasn't the first time I've done battle with myself. More times than I care to remember, I've been my own worst enemy.

The usual wedding toasts were being made. I have heard so many that I confess I don't listen very carefully anymore. But suddenly my ears were at full alert.

A young man with an overly abundant girth was speaking. His subject matter had to do with choices. His honesty grabbed my attention immediately.

He began by reminding us that the choices we make determine our directions in life. Then he spoke about how certain choices brought him into relationship with the couple whom I had just married. He was happy about those choices.

But then in a moment of unusual candor, he said with a wide smile, "I haven't always made the right choices. It's obvious that I've chosen to indulge my love of carbs and forego exercise." Looking around at his laughing audience, he continued, "Not the best choice for my health, but I'm happy with who I am."

My heart warmed in admiration of him. Perhaps one reason I was drawn to him so quickly is that I get so tired of checking everything I eat for the ratio between carbs and proteins and looking for that dirty eight-letter word, *calories*. I envied his freedom from the nutrition chart, which for health reasons had recently become my unwelcome constant companion.

On a recent morning, I was sitting in my usual writing booth at Au Bon Pain when a man looked down at me and said, "That's a mighty defensive posture."

I noticed then that I had leaned back and crossed my arms tightly over my chest. Laughing, I said, "Just fighting with myself over a little sentence structure."

"Well," he said as he exited the restaurant, "I hope you don't lose."

Suddenly my thoughts shifted from sentence structure to a totally different direction. The usual response to an anticipated fight is, "I hope you win." But as I kept thinking about his words, "I hope you don't lose," I wondered if maybe he was on to something. He was an unusually gifted man with an often unique way of looking at the world, and I always enjoyed our conversations.

"Sometimes," I muttered aloud to myself—which I've noticed is also occurring more and more these days—"maybe the best we can hope for is 'not to lose.' Outright victories are not always possible, so maybe avoiding complete losses is also a worthy goal."

Growing up with a mother who could consistently make every food she prepared taste delicious, one of my real joys in life has been the sensual—for me at least—experience of eating good food. I have read that some people have more taste buds than others. I think I have more than my share.

So when I choose to omit certain foods for my health, I guess I haven't lost. But it surely doesn't feel like a victory either.

Maybe that's something of what Paul is talking about in the twelfth chapter of Hebrews: "Let us also lay aside every weight and the sin that clings so closely, and let us run with perseverance the race that is set before us" (v. 1a).

Being "first" doesn't seem to be the main goal or expectation in this verse as it is in some of Paul's other writings. Coming out the victor doesn't appear to be Paul's main emphasis here. The goal is just *getting there—persevering* to the end. The picture that flashes into my mind is of those marathon runners who may cross the finish line an hour after the winner, but they do finish.

That's kind of how I feel when my wife moves the dish of food aside, saying, "Don't you think you've had enough?" It's quite obvious that's a declaration of fact rather than a question. Or worse yet, when Jean prepares my plate and hands it to me with just enough food to keep me alive.

Yep. Just enough to *get there.*

So I guess I haven't lost. But I sure don't feel like a winner either. Oh well. If I keep my weight down, maybe I'll be an easier opponent in those daily battles with myself. "'Perhaps, at the very least,' I tell myself with a deep, drawn-out sigh, 'I can expect not to lose.'"

After all, on the way to Mullinix, getting there is the ultimate goal.

# Smoke and Fire

I was startled to hear my perceptive three-year-old grandson, Austin, tell a friend, "Mother liked that van, but she didn't buy it because it was on fire."

I quickly looked over at Cheryl and said teasingly, "Honey, why did you even look at a van that was on fire?"

Cheryl was speechless for several seconds before she burst into laughter. Seems she did find a van she liked but told her family, which had grown to the size that fit better into a van than a car, "I don't think I want this one because of the smoke."

And, of course, any intelligent three-year-old knows that "where there's smoke, there's fire." The idea that the previous owner had been a heavy smoker, leaving the interior of the van reeking with a burned tobacco smell, never entered Austin's mind.

As smart as my grandson is, three-year-olds do not always see things as they really are. We shouldn't expect that, I guess, since misconceptions occur quite frequently even with adults.

I have never liked the expression "Perception is reality." Now, of course, I know what it means—most people accept their perception of something to be the way it really is. But there's a good chance they're wrong—as wrong as my three-year-old grandson was in believing the van was on fire because his mother said something about smoke.

We are adept at tricking ourselves into seeing and believing a certain way because we either want it to be that way or we are too lazy to look beneath our surface perception.

I vividly remember an incident with one of my classmates in the early years of elementary school. Clara never seemed to have her face washed or her hair combed. Her long blonde hair was always in tangles, and questionable smudges covered her cheeks. Consequently, she was often looked down upon and occasionally bullied.

Our inability to accept differences starts early, I suppose. Does someone being different simply make us uncomfortable, or does pointing out differences give us an opportunity to divert attention from ourselves—with whom we are so often uncomfortable? Or is it the fear that we could become the victim of the bullies for some inadequacy or difference in ourselves?

At any rate, because Clara was not scrubbed as gleamingly clean as the rest of us, she endured many unkind taunts. The incident I remember most vividly, however—and still feel guilty about after all these years—was the ignorance of adults who should have known better. Adults who simply accepted the fact that where there's smoke, there has to be fire. Or maybe adults who merely casually accepted the fact that perception is reality.

I remember the morning Clara came in and proudly showed a smudged paper to our teacher. "I wrote this," she said shyly but proudly, her head lowered and her eyes avoiding contact as she held out the paper.

It was an excellent story to have been "written" by one so young, so the teacher showed it to another teacher, and that teacher showed it to another, until finally it ended up in the hands of the principal.

Somewhere along the trail of telling and retelling, one of the teachers recognized the story as coming from a book she had used in one of her classes. Spelling books back then came with an introductory story illustrating how the words in the spelling list for that week could be used in sentences. That's where this teacher remembered seeing the story.

Consequently, Clara was called up to the teacher's desk and asked, "Are you sure you wrote this?" Clara nodded her head in the affirmative and smiled shyly.

"But one of the teachers found this story in a spelling book." Clara frowned, not understanding why her teacher seemed upset.

"Clara, you can't claim credit for writing something someone else wrote," the teacher said quietly. She was a strict teacher but not unkind. "So I ask you again: Did you write this?"

Turning red and struggling to hold back tears, Clara said quietly, without looking at the teacher, "Yes, ma'am."

"Clara, have you ever heard the word *plagiarism?*"

Of course she hadn't. I hadn't either, and I was one of the best spellers in the class—usually the next to the last standing in our weekly spelling bees. Suzanne McRae was always the winner—as she was in all things involving the brain. Suzanne surprised none of us when she later became a college professor.

"Plagiarism is when you take credit for someone else's writing or idea without giving credit," the teacher concluded. "I'll have to give you a zero for this paper."

A tear crept down each unwashed cheek as Clara turned and hurried back to her seat. Two boys near the back snickered and pointed. "Cheater, cheater," they chanted loud enough for Clara to hear but not loud enough to incur the wrath of the teacher. Bullies are notoriously clever at that kind of thing.

I was not laughing because I was feeling so sorry for Clara and so guilty over my reluctance to step into the conversation when it was easy for me to see that Clara had not meant to say that she had *composed* the story. Rather, she had *written* it in her own hand in the cursive we had been working on in class. Clara was talking about her *penmanship*, not her *authorship*.

While all this whispered conversation was going on among the teachers, I was rehearsing what I could say to help them understand what Clara was meaning. I

*Still Going to Mullinix*

wanted to step up and say, "Clara doesn't mean she wrote it. She means she *wrote* it."
That didn't seem to carry much promise of clarification.

Sadly, at that stage in my education, I lacked the vocabulary to straighten out this unfortunate situation—even though I was also second to Suzanne in the number of library books I read each year. *Compose* was a word I learned later, and somehow *penmanship* did not occur to me.

I confess that in my own shyness, I lacked the courage to confront these clueless adults who held all the authority. I had been taught to respect authority—saying "yes, ma'am" and "no, ma'am"— and struggled at challenging people in positions of power.

But I was totally surprised and mortified by the realization that intelligent adults could not understand something that was so obvious to me, an eight-year-old second-grader.

That reluctance to challenge authority, unfortunately, didn't change until I was well into adulthood. See what I mean about the power of early childhood learning? In my seventies, however, I seem to be challenging *all* authority.

My wife often accuses me of becoming too cynical in my old age toward people in positions of power. Maybe I am, but I've seen a lot during almost fifty years as a pastor while trying to advocate for the powerless in the face of mistreatment from the powerful.

I think it is a little remarkable that after all these years, I still feel some guilt about that early childhood incident when I failed to come to the defense of a classmate who was victimized by grownups who so readily believed that perception is reality.

I have often wondered what happened to Clara and if that incident impacted her life as much as it did mine. By appearance and demeanor, Clara seemed to come from a family that failed to fulfill the need we all have to be loved and accepted as a person of worth.

I wonder if Clara retreated even farther into herself for a lifetime—afraid of making herself vulnerable for fear of being misunderstood and rejected. I have discovered through years of counseling parishioners that much adult behavior had its beginning in similar small childhood moments.

I have much gratitude and admiration for those who love children enough not only to teach them and work with them, but who also take time to see into their hearts. Fred Rogers is still my all-time favorite superhero. All children need advocates like Mister Rogers.

Actually, I think that's something we all need. And as he does for all our needs, God has an answer. Advocacy seems to be one of the central works of the Holy Spirit, as Jesus noted: "'But the Advocate, the Holy Spirit, whom the Father will send in my name, will teach you all things and will remind you of everything I have said to you'" (John 14:26).

Here, Jesus seems to be describing the Holy Spirit as one who "comes alongside" as a helper and a teacher. (Some translations use the word *Helper* rather than *Advocate*.)

It's understandable that a three-year-old—even one as intelligent as my oldest grandson—would assume that where there's smoke, there's fire. That makes perfect sense to a small child.

I find it hard, however, to excuse grownups who fail to see through all the smoke to what is really taking place in people's lives and in the world. That's when "perception is reality" becomes a lazy excuse for not doing the hard work of looking beneath the surface in search for the truth.

Such folks are bound to get lost in the thick smoke and find it difficult to breathe somewhere along the Mullinix road.

# The Right Food

We take our food seriously down in the Piedmont region of North Carolina, where I was born and raised, so I was saddened by the story of a man twenty miles east of my childhood home who shot his wife and son because his wife tried to serve him pork chops for Sunday dinner. I love pork chops for Sunday dinner. (Please note that in North Carolina, "dinner" is the middle-of-the-day meal.)

I always considered it a great privilege to come home after church and sit down to a meal of tender pork chops, mashed potatoes smothered with brown gravy, crowder peas, and green beans cooked with just a spoonful of bacon grease for as long as it takes the water to evaporate. Add some homemade biscuits or yeast rolls and the occasional cake of cornbread, and heaven will have a hard time competing with such joy.

My anticipation of such a meal often caused me to miss the "hymn of invitation" at Calvary Baptist Church, which was usually "Just as I Am" or occasionally "Jesus Is Calling." But since I had "walked the aisle" two years earlier, I didn't feel the invitation applied to me anymore—with one exception.

During the years when an evangelist who was particularly gifted in guilt-producing altar calls led our hot, sweaty, second-week-of-August revivals, I felt like I was still dangling over the fires of hell unless I went forward over and over "just to be safe"—which a number of folks did.

But at a regular Sunday morning service, our pastor was a little more affirming and occasionally even focused on "growth in Christ," so most of the time I felt no real urgency to go back to the beginning of my walk with Jesus and start all over. Just trying to progress from my present stage of discipleship was hard enough.

One positive result of having my response to the hymn of invitation taken care of was that it left my mind free to wander to that meal Mother had begun preparing earlier that morning. As usual, prior to leaving for church, Daddy was rushing us out the door and wondering why it was taking us so long.

"Well, Johnie," Mother would call out from the kitchen, "you only have to get yourself ready. I'm starting dinner to finish when we get home." To Daddy's credit, he always pitched in to help Mother in the kitchen—except, of course, when he was headed for church.

Yes, food was important to those of us who grew up in central North Carolina—especially when there were exceptional cooks like my mother. Mother loved to cook but loved even more watching us enjoy her cooking.

My older sister, Ginny, recently told me about one of her early memories. Our country was nearing the end of WWII, and rationing was in full force. Ginny recalls hearing Mother ask Daddy if he could trade some of his gas stamps for sugar. Mother wanted to bake a cake, and since we lived in town and could walk most places we needed to go, good food seemed much more of a necessity than driving a car.

Like I said, we took our food seriously in my neck of the woods.

Naturally, I was mystified when I read about that man shooting his wife and son over pork chops cooked for his enjoyment. That made no sense—until I read the next paragraph of the front-page article in our county newspaper, *The Montgomery Herald*.

Seems the man had no teeth and he felt his wife should have known he could not "gum" a porkchop into a suitable condition for swallowing.

Two things popped into my mind. First of all, that man had never eaten any of my mother's pork chops. Mother could cook them tender enough for anyone to eat— with or without teeth. The second thing I thought of was that taking food seriously is one thing, but shooting someone over pork chops too tough to eat without teeth is taking it a little too far.

Recent research offers one possible explanation: "Eating the 'right foods' can increase happiness, lessen symptoms of depression and quiet anxiety," one article proclaimed. With no teeth, I guess Mr. Smith hadn't been able to eat the right foods to keep him happy and quiet his anxiety.

But that term *right foods* is a tricky one. When those researchers listed the foods with the "proper nutrients" to "maintain normal brain function," it was obvious they didn't have pork chops and mashed potatoes with thick brown gravy and fluffy buttered biscuits in mind.

So here's the tricky part in my mind. The kind of nutritional foods those anonymous researchers list actually leave me *more* anxious and depressed. Every time I start a new diet with the "right foods," I become irritable and no fun to live with. I know it. Jean doesn't have to keep telling me.

So this is where that "right food" business gets tricky. I get depressed when I go on a diet. I get depressed when I become overweight and my clothes don't fit. So some days I choose to go with the depression that's the most fun. That's worked for me so far. At least I haven't felt the urge to take a shotgun to anyone. Of course, I choose not to test my limits.

After all, Jesus cautions us, "'Watch and pray so that you will not fall into temptation. The spirit is willing, but the flesh is weak'" (Matt 26:41).

I'm not sure Jesus was talking about food, but the principle applies. My spirit is willing to eat the "right foods," but my flesh has a mind of its own—especially when it comes to after-church pork chops.

Come to think of it, my flesh is weak in more ways than I care to mention or even imagine. So pardon me while I pause along this precarious journey to take a deep breath and "watch and pray."

I need a lot of help.

# Disguising Coffee

"The real stuff is the only coffee I can drink," I said while idly conversing with the manager of a local coffee shop as I waited for the "morning blend" container to be refilled and returned to its prominent place at the coffee bar.

"Not me," she replied quickly, with an exaggerated wrinkling of her pretty nose. "I can only drink coffee if it doesn't taste like coffee."

As the coffee urn attendant arrived and placed the freshly brewed morning blend on the counter, I took a quick inventory of the other selections: French roast, French vanilla hazelnut, and, of course, decaf French roast.

According to Google, France was a pioneer in discovering and then importing and exporting this "magical" new drink. But France is not a leader—nor has it ever been a leader—in the production of coffee beans.

Jesus made it clear that being first does not always equate with being the most important when he said, "The last shall be first and the first last." So maybe it's time for the lowly "light roast morning blend" to move to the forefront of all those highfalutin French flavors.

When I walked back to my corner table with the steam rising enticingly from my cup of real coffee—hot enough to burn my tongue, which is the only acceptable temperature for coffee—I reflected on our brief conversation. How many things in life are more satisfying or bearable if they do not taste like the real thing? Life is hard, and we need all the help we can find to get through it, so I have no quarrel with many efforts to disguise harsh reality.

Calling injuries to young children "boo-boos" that are healed with a kiss can be quite beneficial to both children and parents. I have also seen the value of little tricks spouses who have been left alone sometimes use to maintain the feeling of a "presence." Some have found comfort in such things as leaving a place at the table or leaving clothes lying where he or she last left them—until they are strong enough to move on.

However, I'm not as fond of the practice of calling all kinds of behavior—from picking your nose in public to attacking your neighbor with a baseball bat—"inappropriate." Placing all kinds of behavior under one label can easily dilute a sense of healthy guilt and personal accountability if our acts are never bad, wrong, criminal, racist, or bullying.

Reminds me of how accurate a prophet Karl Menninger was a number of years back when he wrote a book titled *Whatever Happened to Sin?*. It has become even clearer than when Menninger wrote his book that "sin" has been replaced with "inappropriate."

When do we cross the line between drinking coffee and consuming an entirely different drink? Can the real thing ever be experienced if our efforts are geared toward making it taste like something else?

That started me wondering how far we can go to make the Christian message palatable to a self-indulgent society, which often labels things "right" or "good" based on how it makes them feel. That is, what new taste do we dare insert into the gospel message in order to attract as many people as possible before we turn it into something entirely foreign to the purity of Jesus's teaching? Jesus said, "'Whoever wants to be my disciple must deny themselves and take up their cross and follow me. For whoever wants to save their life[a] will lose it, but whoever loses their life for me will find it'" (Matt 16:24–25).

Those are demanding words. It costs to follow Jesus. So the church asks, "How do you expect to attract people to the narrow, hard way when they are looking for the broad, easy way?"

I have great admiration for those who find creative ways to entice people to take a fresh look at the Christian faith. But caution must be exercised so we don't alter the real thing and end up with something entirely different.

For instance, there is a brand of Christianity floating around that makes the Christian faith so sugary sweet that folks who have contracted type 2 diabetes risk their lives by embracing it. But the real danger, of course, lies in risking our souls.

It would be impossible for me to count the number of people who have come into our church family—over the thirty-five years I served as pastor—with great enthusiasm, only to drop out a few months later, terribly disappointed.

"It wasn't what I expected, Pastor," they tell me sadly. "The Christian faith promised more than it delivered."

Now it was my turn to be sad. Maybe I had failed them. "Maybe," I replied, "you didn't stick around long enough to get a taste of the real thing. You got a passing whiff of something that smelled good and exciting and followed your nose until the initial aroma faded and you never took a big gulp of the real thing. Maybe you simply 'didn't go far enough for the fun,' as I once heard someone say."

I love the smell of freshly ground coffee beans. I grind my own coffee beans not only for the freshness but for its delectable aroma, which spreads throughout the house. But if I never brewed the coffee and drank a cup, I would never experience the promise of that aroma.

I went back and asked the manager, "How much real coffee have you drunk?"

Laughing self-consciously, she replied, "Well, my parents never drank coffee, and I only had a sip or two when I was in college. But that was enough to convince me that I had to add my own flavor to make it taste good. The real stuff was too bitter for me."

"Ah, just what I thought," I replied. "You have to savor a number of cups of coffee to begin developing a taste for it and experience the real joy of coffee drinking."

"But if I don't like it," she protested, "why keep drinking it?"

"For the potential," I replied quickly. "For the potential. I never drank coffee or particularly liked it until I married and saw how much my wife enjoyed her morning cup of coffee. Watching her convinced me that there must be something more to it than I had previously experienced."

"How long did it take you to like it?" she asked.

"Truthfully, I don't remember when it happened. But somewhere along the way, I crossed the line from being a dubious taster to becoming an authentic coffee drinker. Now I find my morning cup of coffee a comforting and fulfilling way to begin the day."

"So you're saying I haven't really given coffee a chance?"

"Maybe I am," I said as I walked back to my table with a fresh cup.

A few minutes later, my coffeehouse manager friend walked over somewhat sheepishly to my corner where she had often seen me working on a sermon or an essay. That had led to several impromptu discussions during the past months. On many of those occasions, she had expressed her skepticism about religion in general and the Christian faith in particular.

Standing over me now, she waited until I had finished a sentence on my computer and looked up at her. "Were we really talking about coffee just now?" she asked.

"Maybe we weren't," I chuckled, as she turned with a wry smile to wait on another customer.

"I promise you," I called after her, "the real thing can take your breath away." She threw me a skeptical smile as she returned to her duties.

Now it was my turn to be skeptical as I watched her walk away. Would she ever try the real thing and begin her own journey to Mullinix?

Some do. Many don't. I could only hope.

# Starting Small

"For twenty years," he began speaking even before we had time to order our food. That was disappointing because I always think and relate better on a full stomach. "For twenty years," he continued, "I've tried to find God's will for my life. But I don't feel that I'm any closer than when I started." That surprised me because I had known this man as a friend and church member for a long time.

James had called me earlier in the week and wanted to have lunch. It was obvious something was bothering him. I wondered briefly what I had done. After a while, pastors become a little paranoid about such things. We just have to get over ourselves. Not everything is about us.

As I said, I was surprised at James's words because I was aware of this man's quick response to needs of all kind. If anyone was hungry, he was the first to pull out his checkbook.

"What about that?" I asked.

With a dismissive wave, he said, "Aw, that's just a little thing."

The waitress came and took our drink order. I grabbed for the menu, but my friend was too absorbed in our conversation to bother with that. I guessed eating was also "just a little thing" for him.

"And what about that family you kept inviting to church even though they resisted for a long time? Now they're strong leaders in our church. You're the primary reason they're here."

Again, that dismissive wave. "Still just a little thing," he said, growing a little frustrated with my arguments. Well, I told you I was not at my best on an empty stomach.

I continued, "When we deliver meals to needy families, you and your wife are the first to arrive and the last to leave. I've heard that you also care for many of those families throughout the year."

Shaking his head vigorously, he protested, "Pastor, I'm not talking about little things. I'm talking about a ministry that demands a lot. That really challenges me. I've never been able to figure out what it is."

"Maybe I can explain it better if we order first," I replied hopefully.

With a grunt, he picked up a menu and settled on a grilled cheese sandwich. I didn't settle—figuring my ability to offer him a satisfactory answer would increase if I fueled up on a Philly steak and cheese sub with lots of fried onions and peppers.

When the waitress finally left with our orders, I said, "I'm wondering if what you are looking for is based on the wrong concept of what is important." My lunch companion was a highly successful businessman who dealt with big decisions and big deals involving large amounts of money.

"God's will doesn't necessarily involve bigness," I continued between sips of half-and-half iced tea. "Often, I've found it means doing the small thing nearest at hand." In spite of noticing the skeptical look on his face, I plowed ahead.

"Do you remember Jesus's story of the one talent man in Matthew?" I knew James wasn't a biblical scholar but hoped he would recall this famous parable.

James nodded, so I continued, "After giving the three servants differing talents—one five, one three, and the other just one—he went away." I tried to rush the story along when I noticed my friend squirming restlessly. To the first two who told him they had increased that which he gave them, "[the] master replied, 'Well done, good and faithful servant!'" (Matt 25:21). But to the one talent person who had buried it, he said, "'You wicked, lazy servant! ...You should have put my money on deposit with the bankers, so that when I returned I would have received it back with interest'" (Matt 25:26, 27).

Taking another sip of my iced tea, I saw that I still held his attention. Investing and drawing interest, James understood. "I've often thought the main problem of the one talent man was that he did not value it because it was so small. Failed to see its potential." Pausing for a moment, I asked, "What do you think?"

Nodding slowly, my companion muttered, "Could be, could be."

I took his interest as permission to continue. "The little is not little when you place it in God's hands." A slight smile crept onto his face as I said with growing excitement, "What about the five loaves and two fishes that fed 5,000 people? And don't forget that tiny mustard seed that grew into a large tree full of all kinds of potential."

His smile grew wider as he held up his hand. "I get it, Pastor, I get it," he said with a chuckle. "One sermon a week is plenty for me."

When I smiled, he continued thoughtfully, "So you think doing the little things might be important enough to be my mission." It was a statement, not a question.

"I couldn't have said it better myself," I mumbled while taking a large bite of my Philly steak and cheese sub. James was munching quietly around the edge of his tiny grilled cheese sandwich. "He *has* to be on a diet," I thought to myself. "No man as big as he is could possibly eat like that all the time."

After swallowing that first bite, another thought came to me. I told you I think better with a little food in my stomach. "By the way," I said, "doing the little things also helps focus our attention on God and not ourselves."

Frowning, James asked, "What do you mean?"

"Well, when we do something big, everyone's attention is drawn to us. The small things often go unnoticed, except, of course, by God. So we are not tempted by the flattery of others to think too highly of ourselves."

James looked down at the pickle beside his sandwich. "Makes sense," he said, nodding. This man knew what it was like to receive accolades for big decisions that produced big dividends.

"And I have no statistics," I said after a second bite of my comfort food, "but I have a feeling that people find God most often through a little thing someone did or said—a quick word of encouragement, a small act of kindness—things like that."

A tiny light appeared in James's eyes as he nodded. "Now that you mention it, I think that happened to me through a primary class Sunday school teacher in the little country church where I grew up." He paused as his mind wandered to a time long ago. "We had little individual leaflets bound by a white strip of paper glued at the ends." A small smile appeared as he said quietly, "Somehow that teacher smelled like a combination of new paper and Elmer's glue." James's voice almost faded into silence as he concluded, "It was all very comforting."

My lunch companion had stirred my own memories of treasured teachers who helped guide my sprouting faith during my growing up years in Calvary Baptist Church. I didn't have much time to reminisce, however, as James was now attacking his food with much more gusto—the large pickle disappearing in two bites with the grilled cheese sandwich following close behind. That was a sign to me that James was perhaps discovering a new perspective on his mission.

Looking down at my sub, I noticed that even though I had taken several bites, it still looked huge. I was quite pleased that the biblical principle of valuing smallness was not universally applicable.

# Part Eight

A Breathtaking Journey

Is Challenging

# Finding the Center

"**D**ad, why don't we find the cabin first since we have an idea where it's located? Standing on its front steps, it will then be easy to locate the road leading away from the house." Brian, my younger son, spoke with obvious frustration as he looked at me—his face bright red and dripping with sweat from the intense heat of this North Carolina August day.

It was a summer day many years ago when Brian joined me on a challenging hike along Little River. This river is the one I referred to in my first book, *Going to Mullinix*.

*Little* is an apt description of this mostly narrow river that crosses the Piedmont region of North Carolina before finally ending on the northeastern coast of South Carolina.

Approximately 100 acres along the banks of Little River were passed on to my mother from her father, who had inherited it from his family. Thus, it had been a part of our family for several generations.

Brian is the only one of our three children who has—especially in his younger years—enjoyed being in the woods as much as I do. Thankfully, his son, Brent, inherited his father's love of the outdoors. Brent has been my hiking and fishing companion since he was approximately five years of age.

But on the occasion referred to above, Brian and I had just completed one of our more challenging forays along the banks of Little River. The large vines of mostly mountain laurel became so dense in places that our hike became more of a crawl as we dropped to our hands and knees to make our way through low, narrow animal trails.

It was a difficult journey, and we emerged from the blinding undergrowth breathing heavily and with soiled, sweaty clothes clinging to our bodies. Our goal had been to complete our hike near the little cabin my parents had built out of wide oak boards on an isolated peninsula jutting out into the river. We missed our target by a hundred yards or so and were now searching for the road leading to the cabin.

Aggressive vegetative growth—much like that we had just crawled through—had completely engulfed the road leading to the cabin. That was when Brian had his bright idea: "Why don't we go in the direction of the cabin and then find the road leading from its front steps?"

Why hadn't I thought of that? Not only was it the answer to our present dilemma, but in one simple statement, Brian had spoken directly to my reason for journeying to this river through all the thirty-five years I was pastor of Walnut Hills Church in Williamsburg, Virginia.

During those years, I would hear words similar to these: "Pastor, you haven't been yourself lately. Why don't you take a little time off and go down to the river?" Anyone who had been around for a while knew that I would come back renewed and restored from those solitary retreats.

On this occasion, the words of concern were spoken by a deacon, Mitch Thomas, who had been a friend for many years and knew me well enough to tell when I was acting a little off. It isn't very flattering to admit that during most of my years as a pastor, I was a member of that large group of ministers who are much better at taking care of other people than themselves. It was always a humbling realization because I thought I was smarter than that.

However, one advantage to serving as pastor in the same church for many years is that not only do you get to know the people well, but they also get to know you. Such

*Still Going to Mullinix*

knowledge can have its perils, I suppose, but it also makes it possible for us to take better care of each other. Thus, Mitch had noticed I needed some healing river time.

I would begin most mornings of those personal retreats by resting my back against a large oak tree facing the river and praying, "Lord, I can't go any farther. I've exhausted my strength. I'm empty; please fill me. I'm wounded; please heal me." I would not vary from those simple words during the first few days.

How easily we fall into the trap of relying on our own strength. I desperately needed to rediscover that my strength and light must come from the Christ— the center from which all meaningful activity flows.

Matthew tells us, "Now when Jesus saw the crowds, he went up on a mountainside and sat down. His disciples came to him, and he began to teach them. 'Blessed are the poor in spirit, for theirs is the kingdom of heaven'" (Matt 5:1–3).

I understand that the word Jesus uses here for *poor* describes a person who has nothing at all, one who is absolutely destitute. The "poor in spirit" are those who have a deep sense of need. The "poor in spirit" are not fooled into believing they are self-sufficient.

Climbing over the large trunk of a fallen tree and pushing aside thick weeds, Brian and I finally caught sight of the cabin's roof. Excitedly, we stumbled through the heavy undergrowth until we reached the front steps of the cabin.

Just as Brian had predicted, stepping onto the most solid-looking middle front step, we saw the road leading outward.

For me, the feeling was much like the one I always experienced when I returned home from my river time. The roads of purposeful ministry now lay before me— much easier to identify and follow.

In the Bible, rivers most often symbolize movement in the presence of God. No wonder my Little River place was where I was able to catch my breath and find the Center from which all meaningful activity flows.

# The American Dream

Some years back, an alumna of the College of William & Mary called and asked if I would come out to Malibu and perform her marriage ceremony. I do my best to respond to the requests of people who have grown up in our church and college students who have attended Walnut Hills during their college years.

We were especially close to this particular student since we had "adopted" her back in the early 1970s through our church's adopt-a-college-student program. Nancy (not her real name) was also our chief babysitter and barber.

On many Saturday nights, my wife would remind me that I looked too ragged to speak a word from the Lord—even though I showed her a picture of John the Baptist in our children's Bible story book. The matter was sealed when she replied, "Well, you're no John the Baptist."

With that clarified, I would call Nancy, and she would hurry out with her clippers to make her pastor presentable to stand before the Lord on Sunday morning.

So when we received word from California that she wanted Jean and me to come so I could officiate at her Malibu mansion wedding, I could not turn her down. I must confess, however, that I had never quite forgiven her for laughing hysterically at the hairs growing around the outer edges of my ear lobes.

My strong dislike of flying (translation: fear) has been sufficiently documented in other places, so you can imagine something of the affection I felt toward Nancy to make the flight to Los Angeles. After landing at LAX airport, we caught a cab to the Malibu Inn, where a room had been reserved for us.

I had brought my oversized canary yellow swimsuit—the only one I possessed at the time—since Nancy had told us the inn was located on Malibu Beach. However, that oversized canary yellow swimsuit was never unpacked.

I have always liked to explore and get the lay of the land before I venture into unknown territory. I'm glad Paul doesn't include *spontaneity* in his list of spiritual "fruit." That's one fruit that would never have ripened in my soul.

However, minutes after we walked into our luxurious suite, my off-the-chart spontaneous wife already had on her two-piece bathing suit and was wondering why I had not even changed into my bermuda shorts. (You do remember bermuda shorts, don't you? I think I still have a pair on my closet shelf. Come by and take a look if you are into nostalgia.)

When Jean impatiently asked me why I had not changed, I replied, "Have you seen the people on that beach?"

"No, I haven't noticed," she said. "Why?"

"That beach is full of the 'beautiful people.'"

Just a cursory glance had revealed that the women were mostly veiled, anticipating an early morning modeling gig, no doubt. And the men. Well, I bet if I stood on the veranda and yelled "Bubba," not one man would turn his head.

I did that at Myrtle Beach one year when there was actually a Bubba in our group of friends. It was time for lunch, and I went out to the second-floor deck of our rental house—they're decks in Myrtle Beach, verandas in Malibu. Leaning over the rails, I called loudly, "Bubba! Time for lunch!" Half the men on the beach came running.

But Jean wouldn't let me yell here, so we took the elevator to the beach area and slid back into the shadows of a first-floor veranda.

While lying with my back against the outer wall of the inn, I wondered what we could do to blend in better. I suggested to Jean that maybe she could go find a veil and pretend she had a photo shoot the next day. Glancing down the full expanse of my body, she asked, "What are you planning to do?"

"Well," I said, rising to my feet, "while you're looking for a veil, I think I'll grow six inches taller and lose thirty pounds."

In my defense, this was back in the days before I had matured into the understanding that outward appearances are terribly overrated and keeping in shape should have much more to do with health than a desire to be admired by the opposite sex—or any sex for that matter.

But as the weekend progressed, most of my discomfort had to do with the fact that I felt out of place in Nancy's mansion just down the road from Johnny Carson's estate. It was a beautiful home, and I was pleased to have the experience, but, needless to say, I was unaccustomed to such grandeur. When I was shown the spot beside the large outdoor pool where the wedding would take place, I immediately began praying that I would not fall in.

My insecurities had been amplified during the weekend when, while trying to stay out of the way, I kept getting lost in that vast house, once stumbling into a fully furnished beauty shop while Nancy's hairstylist was creating a unique hairdo for the wedding.

Then, just prior to the ceremony, I accidentally wandered into a private session between the bride and groom while he was presenting his most cherished gift to his beloved—a rare bottle of wine from which they were sharing a glass. I apologized for intruding since I was certain that bottle of vintage wine cost more than the bottle of Pepsi my wife and I had shared, along with a hot dog, on our wedding night. (But that's another story.)

Stumbling out of that very private rendezvous, I bumped into Nancy's interior designer, who had moved in for the weekend to make sure there were no disastrous clashing of colors. "By the way," she said, as I apologized for almost knocking her down, "I forgot to ask what you're wearing."

I've always found humor to be a helpful way to deal with uncomfortable situations, so I replied, "Thought I would go with a basic white shirt, held tightly at the neck with a narrow black tie, complemented by black pants, overlaid with your classic black clergy robe accessorized with a flowing white silk stole reaching an inch and a half below my knees and embroidered with a two-inch gold cross three inches above the gold tassels on each end of the stole."

My attempt at humor completely failed on this occasion as the interior designer looked at me with studious seriousness. Finally, she nodded thoughtfully before replying, "I think that will work." But then added, "That's a lot of black. Do you have a white robe?"

"Not with me," I replied. "I usually use the white robe for baptisms."

She remained silent, so I added, "I confess there may be something symbolic in that. I've lost a lot of confidence in the weddings I perform. No matter how hard I try to prepare the couples, nearly half seem to end in divorce."

She replied with a drawn out "Ummmm" before adding, "And you have better luck with your baptisms?"

Who would have thought I could travel all the way across the country from Williamsburg, Virginia, to Malibu, California, only to run into an interior designer who ran a side gig as a religious skeptic?

But she had put me in a reflective mood. I wondered what percentage of those I had baptized in my white robe remained loyal to the faith and the church? Was the percentage more encouraging than that of enduring marital unions? I could quickly recall a sizable number who disappeared soon after their baptism as if the journey of faith—the journey to Mullinix—had been completed.

But the interior designer/religious skeptic was now moving toward the reception hall—I guessed to make sure all the food colors harmonized. I was hoping she liked the combination of brown and white—as in mashed potatoes and gravy.

Well, I'm happy to report that I didn't fall into the Olympic-sized swimming pool and they were married to live happily ever after—at least that was my prayer as we flew home. I always seem to do my best praying on planes, so maybe this prayer would carry some weight.

But I was filled with a pervasive unease.

I have a scrap of paper in my box of scribbled notes dating back to Michael Jordan's first retirement. Jerry Reisdorf, owner of the Chicago Bulls at the time remarked about Jordan, "He's living the American dream. The American dream is to reach a point in your life where you don't have to do anything you don't want to do and can do everything you want to do."

When I read that, I wondered, sadly, when the American dream became just another exercise in self-centeredness and self-indulgence. I was comforted, however, in the confidence that Nancy still held on to the values instilled in her at an early age.

In his letter to the Philippians, Paul thanks them for their concern for him—which evidently resulted in their giving him some kind of gift to help meet his needs.

Paul hastens to add, however, that having his material needs met was not the secret to his contentment: "I am not saying this because I am in need, for I have learned to be content whatever the circumstances.... [Then Paul reveals the true key to his contentment:] I can do all this through him who gives me strength" (Phil 4:11, 13).

Seems Paul had discovered that being filled with the Christ gave all the meaning and purpose and strength he needed. With that, he was content.

Our next to oldest grandson, Christian, tells how he would repeat this verse before taking a foul shot during his high school and college basketball career. Standing at the foul line, Christian would take a deep breath and mutter to himself, "I can do all things through him who strengthens me." Somehow that gave him the calm and confidence he needed to be content with whatever the results might be.

The American dream can still take our breath away when we recover its real meaning—having the freedom to find purpose and fulfillment along the road to Mullinix.

I had confidence that Nancy would find her way.

# No Respecter of Persons

"No, your other left." These words were spoken with a snicker and a condescending tone. The representative of the institution whose venue the bride had chosen for her wedding seemed pleased with her cleverness.

As usual, I was helping my florist-wife with preparations for the upcoming festivities—along with her other helpers. I had just asked the woman assigned to assist us where I could find a particular item. She told me to look in the room to my left.

With so much on my mind, not the least of which was the upcoming ceremony at which I was to officiate, I had inadvertently taken a half step to my right instead of my left. This was the woman's cue to make her derisive comment. "No, your other left," as one might say to a young child just learning his right from his left.

Now, that might seem like something too small to even mention—much less write about. But this was an instance of adding another straw to that camel's back, who, strong as he is, does have a load limit.

It was not unusual. In fact, I had almost come to expect this attitude from people in positions of authority. Certainly not all were this way. In fact, most were gracious and helpful. A surprisingly high percentage, however, fell into the category of this woman, who felt her position entitled her to treat those under her in whatever manner she chose.

I never liked it, of course. I did, however, learn to appreciate those experiences for helping me walk in another's shoes for a few minutes and feel just a little of what it means to be ignored or counted as of little importance. For that I was grateful.

Empathy is an important quality for a pastor.

I have not experienced a lot of that "you're of little value" treatment in my life. I was fortunate to grow up in an affirming family atmosphere. Also, in most places, ministers/pastors are still treated with a certain amount of respect. To top it off, I am white and educated.

At the wedding on this day, as most days, my wife had been treated with the utmost respect because she was the expert on wedding flowers and table arrangements. Jean was the one with authority and position of her own while I was clearly the errand boy—the "gofer"—standing on one foot, blissfully ignorant and helpless, awaiting instructions on where to go and what to do, struggling to learn simple things like my right from my left. A common laborer to be ignored or counted as unworthy of receiving notice or respect.

But now it was time. (God forgive me for enjoying this part too much.) Time for me to switch roles. So I retired to a private room to clean up, change from my dirty work clothes, and put on my robe and white stole with the gold-embroidered crosses. I placed my sweatpants and faded "UNC 2005 National Champions" t-shirt in a plastic bag to retrieve after the ceremony.

As I emerged from the changing room, I intentionally walked by my privileged superior and spoke congenially—ostentatiously nodding at her, almost bowing. Her face paled, and her eyes grew wide as she temporarily lost her way—clearly recalling her treatment of me while also trying to remember what she had said during the previous few hours.

I was not who she thought I was, and she was thrown into a terrible confusion since "who she thought I was" was the determining factor of how she should treat me.

But now, suddenly, I was the one in charge, the "officiant," the clergyman, the one with position, and it threw her people-value system completely off balance.

I have always enjoyed—probably much too much for a professed humble pastor—poking holes in people's pretentious bubbles. Maybe one of them, here and there, will wake up to the effects of their demeaning attitudes.

But I can't claim my motives on that day were entirely pure. Part of my actions, I am certain, had its source in my core cynicism of folks in positions of authority—whether that authority came from wealth or "class" or office—fed through many sad observations and experiences over many years. So I feel bad about feeling good at my smug revenge—small as it was—because Jesus seemed to be saddened by my kind of behavior. I knew I was supposed to turn the other cheek, but I felt both cheeks had been stung rather severely and I was running out of good will.

But you do understand, I hope. I'm still on the way to Mullinix—that place of mature Christlikeness. I haven't arrived yet. And, besides, I do have a prooftext to justify my behavior.

By the way, I have discovered that prooftexts are mighty handy to justify most any behavior the human species has ever devised. You just have to search the scriptures long enough and with the proper prejudice.

James writes, "My brothers and sisters, believers in our glorious Lord Jesus Christ must not show favoritism. Suppose a man comes into your meeting wearing a gold ring and fine clothes, and a poor man in filthy old clothes also comes in. If you show special attention to the man wearing fine clothes and say, 'Here's a good seat for you,' but say to the poor man, 'You stand there' or 'Sit on the floor by my feet,' have you not discriminated among yourselves and become judges with evil thoughts?" (Jas 2:1–4).

I was first introduced to F. Scott Fitzgerald back in an American literature class at the University of North Carolina in the early 1960s. Fitzgerald famously talked about how the rich are different from you and me. One of those differences lies in the area of expectations—they *expect* to be coddled and admired and respected.

But I was thinking the other day how the rest of us are partially responsible for that expectation. If we treat the rich or well-positioned differently, in the manner James describes, that only enables their natural tendencies toward entitlement and selfishness and self-centeredness.

On the other hand, if we pass by or ignore the not-rich, the not-powerful, the not-well-positioned, are we not doing the much more serious thing of ignoring the Christ, who very clearly identified with such folks? "'Truly I tell you, whatever you did for one of the least of these... you did for me'" (Matt 25:40).

If we are having trouble finding the Christ or imitating the Christ, maybe a first step would be waking up to the presence and the value of the poor, the ragged, the imprisoned, the powerless.

What such folk can teach us about the Christ might just take our breath away.

# Being Too Careful

"You be real careful now!" had become a popular chorus as I was gathering my belongings to return home after another visit with my family in the small town of Mt. Gilead, North Carolina. My father had passed away a few years prior, but I still made regular trips to spend time with Mother.

It was a very musical group gathered in Mother's den—my sister Donna and three nieces: Michelle, Brooke, and Jackie. So the chorus was well-harmonized.

"You be real careful." I had heard those same words a little earlier from the woman who cares for Mother each day. I had never heard her sing, but she had a very musical way of talking. "Now you be re-aaal care-a-ful goingggg home, ya heaa-ah-hh?" Nodding her head vigorously for emphasis, she added, "They's some baaa-addd accideeents happen out thereeeee. Yeaaa-aah." It was fascinating to me that each word seemed to dance up and down the musical scale with syllables added where necessary.

A little earlier, an aunt had called me, saying, "The roads are going to be real crowded out there today, Jerry. You be careful."

I was fast becoming paranoid. Did they know something I didn't? Was this a mass premonition of impending doom that somehow had bypassed my notice? I have always felt I have a strong intuition concerning the future. My daughter, Cheryl, often checks in to ask what I am feeling before she takes a long trip. But I had felt no particularly strong vibes on this day.

I was wondering, however, if I should even begin the journey home. Perhaps I should just hunker down, call Jean, and tell her that I was going to wait it out and start home when it was safer.

But I knew that if she asked when that would be, I would have no answer. Is there ever an answer for that? Is there ever an answer for "When is it safe?"

I concede that the newspapers had been saying all week that Wednesday was going to be the most heavily traveled day on the highways. Not only was it the day before Thanksgiving, but there was a lingering fear of air travel even five years removed from 9/11. AAA had said almost ninety percent of travel was going to be by car this holiday week—the highest percentage on record for a Thanksgiving week.

And you can't be too careful, can you?

Just a couple days prior to the Passover, Mark tells us that Jesus stopped by the house of Simon the leper in Bethany, where an unexpected thing happened: "While [Jesus] was in Bethany, reclining at the table in the home of Simon the Leper, a woman came with an alabaster jar of very expensive perfume, made of pure nard. She broke the jar and poured the perfume on his head" (Mark 14:3).

That would seem like a beautiful thing to do. But Mark says the disciples didn't see it that way. They reacted with anger: "'Why this waste of perfume? It could have been sold for more than a year's wages and the money given to the poor'" (Mark 14:4a–5).

Evidently, the disciples felt this woman (whom some have called Mary), was simply not being careful enough.

But Jesus stepped in, saying, "'Leave her alone"…"Why are you bothering her? She has done a beautiful thing to me'" (Mark 14:6).

Was Jesus saying we *can* be too careful?

No doubt it's a dangerous world. One thing I have learned over many years as a pastor is that life can be altered dramatically in a moment. So proper caution in a world full of willful evil and sudden crises and tragedies is necessary. We need to be careful. But I guess the problem arises when our caution spreads unnecessarily into all areas of our lives—especially to the arena of discipleship.

You know what I think was happening in this scene Mark gives us? Jesus knew that very soon he would be going up to Jerusalem. Jerusalem was full of people eager to kill him.

Perhaps Jesus sensed that their awareness of growing danger was making the disciples overly cautious. *Too* careful, maybe? So careful they were moving into the most dangerous place of all—the place of a cautious, carefully measured-out discipleship.

"Let her alone," Jesus said. "She has performed a good service for me."

A couple hours following all the dire warnings, I climbed into my car and headed home. I planned to exercise the proper caution, but if I gave into all my fears, I would never begin the journey home—or maybe any journey.

Especially the seemingly reckless, breathtaking Mullinix journey of saving my life by losing it for Jesus's sake.

# The Dangers of Preaching

They did not look like your usual mob as they walked purposefully toward me, surrounding me on all sides.

All of them were well-dressed—some of the men wore ties and jackets. A few of the women wore colorful dresses, while others were in more formal dark colors. Both the men and women gave off the pleasant aroma of expensive colognes and perfumes. There was not a hint of the rank, acrid odor of sweat and hate usually emanating from an angry mob.

Still, I couldn't help but take an involuntary step backward as they came at me with unhappy faces and words piggybacking onto each other, expressing a deep displeasure over the sermon I had just preached.

All of this took place on July 3, 2006—a big day for the historic town of Yorktown, Virginia, and for Yorktown Baptist Church. As you would expect, those people take their history seriously. So, naturally, that close to July 4, I felt obliged to delve into a little history in my sermon.

I talked some about the achievement of our independence by way of the last major battle of the American Revolutionary War at Yorktown on the battleground just a few hundred yards from the Baptist church. What I had said about that decisive battle was that General Washington began *gathering* all his troops in August 1781, preparing to march toward Yorktown.

What they heard me say was that the *decisive* battle of the revolution was *fought* in August 1781. Every soul in that worship service knew that the last major battle occurred October 19, 1781.

So that misunderstanding was why, immediately after the service, I was cornered by a six-member tag team of historical interpreters and history buffs who proceeded to give me a rather emphatic history lesson.

"If you had gone to York High School, you would *never* forget October 19," one woman exclaimed in a voice I had heard from many of my schoolteachers. Her declaration was accompanied by the vigorous nodding of heads and murmurs of approval.

"Well," I replied meekly, "I went to Mt. Gilead High School in North Carolina, but I was born on October 19, so I do tend to remember that date during most years." Smiling weakly, I continued, "I was, of course, born a few years after 1781." My feeble attempt at humor did not deter in the slightest the exasperation of these historical soldiers.

However, after a few moments of explanation and my apology for offending their sense of history, they apologized for the intensity of their objections. One sympathetic woman straightened my tie, and another tried to smooth the wrinkles out of my suit jacket.

Every once in a while, I am reminded of the dangers of preaching. This was clearly one of those times in which the risk of being misunderstood was dramatically demonstrated. People do not always hear what you intend to say.

I must take partial blame when I am not as clear as I should be. I had quite obviously failed on this occasion. Then, too, I sometimes forget to follow the advice of my first boss and mentor, Dr. Richard Stephenson, pastor of Columbia Baptist Church in Falls Church, Virginia.

I was just out of the seminary in the late 1960s when I expressed anxiety over preaching to that large congregation, which included top government people and experts in many areas. Dr. Stephenson listened sympathetically and then gave me this advice: "Try not to venture too deeply into non-theological areas like science or the economy, where someone there knows far more than you on the subject." He added with a chuckle, "They'll call you out. It's happened to me."

Most of the time, I've followed his advice. But occasionally, like at Yorktown on that Fourth of July weekend when I dove into deep historical waters right in the middle of accomplished history sharks, I have failed—at my peril—to heed his guidance.

Now, I knew those good people at Yorktown were not going to attack me physically. I wasn't so sure about the man who charged me just prior to the last note of the "hymn of commitment" following an eleven o'clock worship service at Columbia.

I was preaching on one of those rare occasions when Dr. Stephenson was out of town. Again, it was in the late 1960s, when the tension and conflict of that turbulent civil rights time had just that week climaxed in widespread burning and looting on the streets of Washington, DC—just six or seven miles across the bridge from our church.

Being recently graduated from the seminary, I was filled with the idealism of the young, ready to "tell it like it is" in no uncertain terms, whatever the circumstances. That morning I had preached on forgiveness and loving even your enemies.

I had preached on that subject before in that same pulpit. But on that first occasion the subject matter had been delivered in the abstract. It's pretty easy to be a Christian and agree with Jesus's teachings in the abstract.

But on this morning, following a night of pillaging and burning, the principles of forgiving and loving became intensely real and concrete. Like I said, I was young and naive and convinced you could actually apply Christian principles to real-life situations in any environment.

The man charging toward me with eyes blazing and fists clenched did not think so.

"Jerry!" he exclaimed loudly. (After all, he and I were on a first-name basis.) "I hated what you said!"

"What part was that?" I asked in what sounded to me like a fairly normal tone, even though I had temporarily stopped breathing. Shock can often make you sound much calmer than you feel.

When he told me what had so deeply offended his sensitivities, I replied, "You know I was paraphrasing Jesus at that point, don't you?"

"Well, I don't care!" the red-faced man sputtered so violently that a few droplets of spit were launched in my direction as I involuntarily stepped back. (I am thankful we weren't in the middle of the 2020 coronavirus pandemic—what with all those wet droplets flying around.) "I don't think Jesus should have said that either," he continued. "It's impossible to do! I just can't do it!"

"I'm not sure I can either," I replied. I paused and swallowed deeply in an effort to maintain my composure. "But don't you think we are expected to try?" He didn't reply immediately, so I added, "Maybe sometimes he's pleased with our best efforts—even when we fail."

Still mumbling and shaking his head angrily, his body continuing to tremble, the man finally stepped aside to give me just enough room to escape down the long aisle toward the front doors of the sanctuary.

Sometimes we preachers get in trouble because we are misunderstood. At other times we get in trouble because we are understood too clearly. Jeopardy lies in either direction.

But here's one of the miracles of the Christian faith. That charging bull of a man and I became close friends in the weeks following that eventful Sunday morning. Only by grace.

And those good people at Yorktown Baptist? A few weeks later, they asked me to come back and preach again, which of course I was happy to do—although I did carefully avoid any mention of historical events. Then, a few months later, following several additional preaching stints with them, they asked if they could talk to me about becoming their interim pastor. I have no doubt I would have accepted their kind offer if I had not already been in conversation with another church. I love the Yorktown area, not far from my home in Williamsburg, and I had grown quite fond of the people of Yorktown Baptist.

The journey toward Mullinix—toward mature Christlikeness—is filled with numerous hazards and risks of all kinds. But John gives us this promise: "This is the victory that has overcome the world, even our faith. Who is it that overcomes the world? Only the one who believes that Jesus is the Son of God" (1 John 5:4b–5).

You don't need a man charging down a church aisle with clinched fists for that promise to leave you breathless.

# Where's Papa?

"Where's Papa?" The voice of our three-year-old grandson coming from the front foyer caused me to hesitate and look back toward the source of the voice. I knew Brent wasn't asking about my present location since he had just seen me turn the corner into the kitchen.

It happened every Advent season since 1996. During winter of that year, Walnut Hills very generously gifted us with a trip to the Holy Land on the occasion of our twenty-fifth anniversary with the church.

Jean and I had purchased an olive wood creche when our tour group stopped for a quick visit in Bethlehem. Each year, the Christmas season arrived at our house when Jean unpacked that manger scene and carefully arranged it on a table in the front foyer. The only difference this year was the addition of a three-year-old grandson who had been with us several days a week for all three of his years. This year, he was old enough to be very interested in the nativity scene.

Brent watched in rapt attention as Nana explained each piece: "Here is Mary, and beside her is Jesus's father, Joseph. Over here, a little farther back, are the shepherds." Brent's eyes were wide and shining as he stared at each additional piece placed in the wooden Christmas scene. "Then, behind the shepherds are the wise men bringing their gifts to the baby Jesus."

As he moved a little closer, almost bumping the table with his nose, a puzzled frown appeared on Brent's face.

"What's wrong?" Jean asked.

Surveying the scene even closer, Brent asked softly, "Where's Papa?"

That unexpected question was what had brought me to a sudden stop.

Several days a week since he was three months old, I had met Brent and his dad, our youngest son, Brian, at 5:30 in the morning. Brian opened the Williamsburg Indoor Sports Complex at 6:00 and then picked Brent up at 2:30 in the afternoon on his way home in Newport News. Brent's mother, Shelley, was a local schoolteacher for special needs children. Over the years, I have marveled at her love and selfless devotion to those children.

In those days of his infancy, I would put Brent to bed each morning in what later became his playroom and then lie on the couch close by so he would see me immediately upon waking. Consequently, I had a place in most scenes of his early life.

But suddenly I was missing from this Christmas scene, and it bothered him.

As I reflected on Brent's question, it began to bother me too. Where was I? How many times had I been absent from the Christmas scene?

The Christmas season is always so frantic around a church that I have often found myself caught in a whirlwind just to keep up with my pastoral responsibilities. I was also amazed at how often some of the most serious illnesses within our church family occurred during the Christmas season. (But that's another story.)

So I suddenly realized three-year-old Brent's question had validity: "Where *is* Papa?" How often had I paused during the Christmas season to kneel before the manger? Yes, where was I in the manger scene?

That unexpected question also took me back to another season. It was a summer place, a summer scene. We had gathered with family at our once-every-two-years vacation at Emerald Isle Beach.

A couple family members felt I had let my beard—which they had never liked anyway—get a little too bushy and hot-looking for the beach. So in a moment of weakness, unknown to anyone, I had sneaked off to the bathroom and shaved my face clean.

When I walked back into the great room of our rented house, where all the family was gathered, the reaction was totally unexpected. My two sons, Chris and Brian, looked completely startled before collapsing on the floor in hysterical laughter.

For one thing, they had not seen me clean-shaven for fifteen years or so. Also, the skin under my beard was several shades whiter than the part of my face that had been exposed to the sun. I had noticed that it looked a little strange when I was shaving, but I had not expected this degree of hilarity.

But the thing that touched me the most was the reaction of my seven-year-old granddaughter, Kayla. A look of confused sadness filled her face as she stared at me before proclaiming, "You're not my Papa."

Even though I carefully assured her that nothing had changed except my face, she could not be persuaded or consoled. For the remainder of the day and evening, she avoided me as if I had a contagious disease.

Much to my relief, however, the next day, Kayla began slowly warming up to me as we engaged in a variety of activities together. Then, finally, as we gathered for our nightly indoor games—always led by my son-in-law, Steve—Kayla began gradually accepting me back into the family. I like to think that even though my physical appearance had been altered, the essence of my "papahood" was showing through. Kayla began recognizing that I still possessed the heart of her Papa.

Kayla is now a very open and accepting woman of twenty-nine who persistently looks beyond outward appearances to the person underneath. I like to think that maybe that week at the beach was a small, mustard-seed-sized contribution to the kind of lifestyle that has led her to look at people from the inside out.

I hope, too, that Brent, who is now thirteen and my constant fishing and hiking companion, can find his Papa in the Christmas scene. After all, that's what our Lord's birth was all about: "The Word became flesh and made his dwelling among us. We have seen his glory, the glory of the one and only Son, who came from the Father, full of grace and truth" (John 1:14).

God showed up in human flesh in Bethlehem so that he might show up in all places through those who choose to follow him.

If, along our journey, we can just keep kneeling before the manger, that breath-taking miracle can happen again and again.

# Aging Gracefully?

I was crouched in my usual corner at Panera Bread, busy at my computer, when I glanced up to see a slightly-past-middle-aged couple staring at me.

Finally, they walked over and stood at the corner of my table. "We apologize for staring, but we thought we recognized you as a local pastor," the woman explained.

Returning her smile, I replied, "Well, you're partly right. I was a local pastor for thirty-five years."

"We thought so," the man said as they both smiled triumphantly. "Which church?"

"Walnut Hills," I said quickly. I am always happy to affirm my association with that good church.

The woman studied my face carefully as she quickly scrolled through her bank of memories. Finally, she said, "Were you there *before* or *after* Jerry?" I had been there so long that people had a tendency to classify church events as happening before or after my tenure.

I hated to answer that question because I knew it would embarrass her. So as gently as I could, I replied, "Ma'am, I *am* Jerry."

Squirming like a little girl caught smearing on her mother's lipstick, the woman lost her smile and turned a deep red. I started crying.

Stammering in an effort to find the right apology, each of them muttered something about not seeing me in probably fifteen years or so—which was about how long I had been retired.

But had I really changed that much? Even in fifteen years?

Aging is a deceptive thing—much more evident to others than to ourselves. When we see our face in the mirror each day, we scarcely notice the little changes creeping in—little changes that, over time, join to yield a big change.

Maybe this is a good time to tell you that I have never been fond of the phrase *aging gracefully*—especially when my arthritic right thumb makes it difficult to open jars with ease, even after repeatedly abusing the stubborn container on the edge of a hard surface. Or when I am struggling to rip into an unusually stubborn bag of nuts and one of my sons casually takes it from me and, with one swift motion, tears it open with ease.

My reaction at such times can in no way be characterized as "graceful"—even as I quickly explain that my arthritic right hand is no doubt the result of filling thousands of legal pads with sermon notes and manuscripts in the decades before computers.

A church friend of mine, Jim Liddel, and I are constantly updating our levels of "progressive aging." First, of course, are the energetic years of youth and vitality. That needs no explanation. Next comes middle age and a slightly noticeable diminishing of energy. Then comes the post-middle age stage, when everyone starts saying, "You look good."

I have become accustomed to people who have not seen my wife and me for a number of years saying, "Jean, you haven't changed a bit!" Then, glancing over at me, they continue—much less enthusiastically—"Jerry, you're looking good." (Note: when people keep assuring you that you look good, you're not looking good.)

One day, in the church hallway, Jim stopped me and added another level of aging: "My daughter called and said we should consider moving in with her. I've inserted that as the fourth stage of aging."

"Let me tell you about something that happened to me yesterday," I said. "Maybe we can make room for this on our list." Jim looked up attentively as I continued.

"I was checking out at a local grocery store when the friendly young woman who had just bagged my groceries said, 'Can I walk you to your car?'"

I thanked her but assured her I could make the short trip across the parking lot on my own with two small bags of groceries. She looked at me dubiously and said, "I don't know. Those bags seem a little heavy." I appreciated her kindness but resisted a sudden urge to slap her youthful face.

Laughing, Jim said, "That would make a good fifth level of aging." A couple days later, I was sitting in church waiting for the service to begin when Jim walked back to my pew, smiling.

"You remember that young lady in the grocery store who asked if she could help you to your car?" I nodded, and he continued, "Well, my wife was asked the same thing recently. She declined and said, 'My husband is waiting for me over there.' The woman took a good look at me, paused, then turned back to my wife and said again, 'May I walk you to your car?'"

After we both stopped laughing, Jim continued, "But I have another stage of aging."

"What's that?" I asked.

"The other day, I was visiting a friend in an assisted living facility. When I started to leave and looked around for the exit, a nurse stopped me and asked, 'Could I help you back to your room?'"

I doubled over in laughter as I remarked, "Yep, visiting an assisted living facility and they try to keep you certainly qualifies as another stage of aging."

"I keep telling myself she probably saw my handsome face and just wanted to get me in a room alone," Jim said chuckling.

"That reminds me," I said. "Last week, I stopped by Ace Hardware following a funeral I had just conducted. I was still dressed in my navy blue suit with a light blue shirt and pink tie." Jim was smiling expectantly. "So when I checked out, the young

*Still Going to Mullinix*

cashier looked me up and down and said, 'You look cute.' Now, in my younger years, I would have accepted that as a compliment. 'Hey! This pretty young lady thinks I'm hot!' But somehow her tone sounded a little condescending. Such as, 'This old man is trying so hard I need to humor him.' Am I being paranoid, Jim?"

Unable to contain his laughter, even though the pastor was standing to begin the service, Jim replied, "No, I think you're reading the situation perfectly. That has to be at least a couple stages beyond 'you're looking good.'" His shoulders still shaking with laughter, Jim took a seat on the pew in front of me as the pastor began the "call to worship."

Following the morning worship, thinking our little game had gone on long enough, Jim asked if we could agree on the final stage: "They sure laid him out nicely, didn't they?"

"That has to be the last one, I guess," I said, chuckling.

My mother used to say, "Jerry, it takes a lot of courage to grow old." At times, I've questioned whether I have the required courage, furiously trying to ignore every stiff joint and new back pain.

Old Caleb has helped me some. At eighty-five (I need to tell you that's several years older than me), Caleb got up one morning, stretched, yawned loud enough to wake his wife, and said, "'I am still as strong today as the day Moses sent me out; I'm just as vigorous to go out to battle now as I was then. Now give me this hill country that the LORD promised me that day. You yourself heard then that the Anakites were there and their cities were large and fortified, but, the LORD helping me, I will drive them out just as he said'" (Josh 14:11–12).

On a quiet morning I can still hear the echo of his wife's laughter: "As strong as you were forty-five years ago? Give me a break, you old fool!"

But maybe there's something here besides Caleb's defiant, silly-sounding words.

Forty-five years earlier, Caleb and Joshua had come back from scouting out the promised land with a minority report of two declaring it *was* possible to defeat the giants who inhabited the land. Seems they had seen something the other scouts who counseled *against* invasion failed to see: "The Lord will be with us."

Mountains are always before us. As we age, some of them loom bigger and bigger. Yet if we hold fast to the conviction that "the Lord will be with us," perhaps life at any age can be negotiated with meaning and purpose and joy.

I hope that's what folks mean when they talk about "aging gracefully"—still eagerly searching for meaning and purpose in their lives, rather than merely lying on the couch and acquiescing to whatever the passing years bring.

I can live with that even if my breathing becomes a little labored as I hurry to keep up with my grandson on our long hikes.

Note: While writing this piece at Au Bon Pain—my other writing "hole"—I overheard a woman say that her grandson, who had just turned twenty-one, told her he would like to reverse the aging process and also the numbers of his age to twelve instead of twenty-one.

I suddenly realized something I had been overlooking. Aging is not only a phenomenon of the elderly. No matter how many years we've been on this earth, the process of aging is always at work. The elementary student who moves into middle school is aging. The high school student who goes away to college is aging. The college student who is moving out into the adult world is aging. And on and on it goes as long as life goes on.

We are all in this business of aging together. So maybe I should try harder to adopt the perspective of the person I heard say recently, "Aging is a gift."

I snickered at that when I first heard it. But maybe aging *is* a gift if we learn to use it like old Caleb—finding *meaning* and *purpose* and *joy* at every stage along the Mullinix journey because "the Lord will be with us."

Let me assure you that my shortness of breath that comes with that thought is the result of wonder and not the effect of age. I think.

# Does They Have a Muvver?

His small, frowning face and tense body revealed an almost overwhelming anxiety. But his fear was not for himself as he looked up and cried, "Does they have a muvver?"

My wife and I were returning home from a Nags Head vacation a few years ago. Just before our departure, someone mentioned an excellent breakfast place we needed to check out. I rarely pass by an eating establishment where I can find my favorite meal of the day.

Our difficulty in finding a place to park immediately told us that lots of other vacationers had also discovered this place. Then, when we entered the restaurant, we were startled to see that the line of customers wound all the way to the front door.

Jean immediately turned to leave, but I grabbed her arm. "Wait a minute! Do you smell that food?" The aroma of North Carolina sausage and smokehouse-cured bacon balanced with the sweet smell of waffles and maple syrup (their specialty) filled the air, transfixing me in place.

Afraid I would burst into tears and embarrass her once again if she insisted on leaving, Jean conceded. So as we took our place at the end of the long line, two young children, a boy and girl, their eyes wide with alarm, rushed by us, haphazardly racing from one corner of the restaurant to the other in a panicked search.

Following close on their heels was a small boy. He was younger than the two children who had just passed us, but his blue eyes showed the same panic. Stopping in front of us—we probably reminded him of his grandparents—he looked up into our faces and gave that desperate cry, "Does they have a muvver?"

Glancing in the direction I had last seen the two children race, I saw them pulling up chairs next to their parents. I was happy I could look down at the frantic little fellow and say, "They sure do have a muvver. And they just found her!"

Almost collapsing in relief, the little boy turned and ran hurriedly back to his own mother standing near the front of the line.

Still smiling at the concerned little boy's question, I began reflecting on how that is one of life's most important questions: "Does they have a muvver?" Do they have someone to watch over them? To care for them? To give them a place to belong? Someone to give them a home and direction in this lonely universe where we so easily lose our way and feel we have been orphaned?

Glancing over at the table where the anxious little boy and his mother were now seated, I could not help but wonder why he had such strong empathy for the two temporarily lost children. Had he lost the grip on his mother's hand in a large store and frantically searched each aisle before finding her? Had he spent time in the foster care system before finding someone who became his "forever" mother?

Or maybe, like me, he had experienced an illness during which his mother became his only lifeline.

I was around five years old when I contracted a serious case of measles. At times, lying in the bed, I would call out that I could not breathe. That was when Mother, who never left my side, would sit on the edge of the bed and lift me to a sitting position in order to dispel the paralyzing feeling of suffocation.

Back in 1945 measles was quite prevalent and critical. The measles vaccine was not licensed until 1963, so in the mid-1940s millions of people contracted the disease, with hundreds of deaths attributed to measles each year.

An elderly relative stopped by Pa-Pa's house, where we were temporarily living while our own home was under construction. Later, I heard that the relative had contracted measles, no doubt from me, and had died.

Imagine my fear when, after I had finally recovered, Mother was also diagnosed with measles and lingered near death for several days. One frightening image I have of that time is our family doctor, Dr. Vernon Andrews, standing outlined in the door of Mother's darkened bedroom with a colleague he had called in as a consult. Their gloomy faces told me they had exhausted all their treatment options.

I felt terribly guilty about the elderly relative who had died, but I knew I could not live with the burden if my own mother died after catching measles from me. Thankfully, after a painstakingly long struggle, Mother recovered, although it took her a long time to regain her strength.

Many years later, when I had a family of my own, I had traveled down from Williamsburg to visit my parents for a couple days. I was sitting at the bar separating the kitchen from the dining room, watching Mother at her usual place—standing over the white electric cook stove—when a question suddenly popped into my mind. We had been quietly talking about family and memories of past years when our mutual bout with measles came up.

"Mother," I said suddenly, "you knew the risks. How could you hold me up day after day as I breathed those menacing germs into your face?"

Thoroughly surprised by my question, Mother paused briefly from her stirring and turned to face me. With a slight shrug before turning back to the stove, she said, "I was your mother."

It was that simple for her. In her mind, that was just what mothers did. A mother was supposed to be willing to risk her life in an effort to save the life of her children.

We're most accustomed to seeing Paul as a zealous missionary or a courageous theologian who never shirked the big questions about God and the tenets of Christianity even in the face of hostile opposition.

So these words from 1 Thessalonians may carry something of a surprise: "We were like young children[a] among you. Just as a nursing mother cares for her children, so we cared for you. Because we loved you so much, we were delighted to share with you not only the gospel of God but our lives as well" (2:7b–8).

So deep was Paul's affection for those Thessalonians that he gave not only the words of the gospel but his very life—his own soul.

Paul sounds a lot like a mother, doesn't he? I suppose that's one reason we dare call the Christian church a family. Following Paul's guide, we say to each other, "I am your mother. I am your father. I am your brother. I am your sister."

That gives me the help I need to continue the often difficult journey to Mullinix. Family to hold me up—no matter what the cost to themselves—when I find it difficult to breathe.

# Death by Addiction

Pausing halfway through the bedroom window, I was startled to hear a siren out on Route 5. Hurriedly, I jerked my dangling legs inside, landing with a painful clatter on a half-dozen empty beer cans. I listened carefully to determine if the siren was heading in my direction.

It was the middle of a fall afternoon, so I had assumed that most people in the nearby houses would be at work. But I was also fully aware that someone could be watching and would surely call 911 to report a middle-aged man breaking and entering through a side window of their neighbor's house. Neighborhood Watch was very active in that area.

They had no way of knowing that I was there because of a mother's love.

Satisfied that the siren was moving on down John Tyler Highway, I proceeded to carry out the worried mother's request. She had reached me at my church study when I was preparing for a round of afternoon visits.

Her voice was pleading. "Jerry, I hate to ask you to do this. But I can't get Paul on the phone." She paused a moment to calm her trembling voice. "I've been calling him half the night and all morning. I just want to know if he's alive." Those last words were spoken with a muffled sob.

Her husband had given up on their son after many years of extensive counseling and expensive rehab. I remembered their recent experience with one highly recommended treatment facility that had cost thousands of dollars, which the family had taken out of its retirement fund.

On the day he was released, Paul went to the home he now occupied alone—his wife had finally given up and left—and started binge drinking. After months in the rehab facility, he had remained sober just long enough to go to the nearest store and purchase several cases of Budweiser—at least that was the label on the dozens of empty cans I now saw scattered on the bedroom floor, trailing on into the living room.

Climbing to my feet from the painful spot on the floor where I had so ungracefully landed, I walked over to the rumpled bed, where Paul lay fully clothed, spread-eagled, on top of the covers.

I had been unable to detect any up and down movement of his chest when I had peered through the bedroom window earlier. Staring down at him at closer range, however, I could detect a barely discernible movement. I was relieved that, at least this time, his mother's worst fears were not realized.

I leaned over, shaking him and calling loudly, "Paul! Paul!" It took a lot of shaking and loud calling before his eyes flickered slightly as he gave out a low moan.

I renewed my shaking and shouting until I decided to give him a moment to gather himself. Walking into the kitchen, where I found a container of plastic trash bags in a cabinet drawer next to the filthy sink, I began filling the bags with the empty beer cans—being sure to make enough noise that it would continue to rouse Paul.

After filling several trash bags and stacking them in a kitchen corner, I returned to Paul's bed with more shouting and shaking. Finally, his moaning turned into an erratic flailing of his arms as Paul tried to push me away. When I refused to move, his eyes opened into little slits, followed by a growing awareness as he blinked rapidly.

"J-Jerry?" he finally mumbled, trying to sit up. He knew me well, of course. I had been his pastor since he was a small boy, baptized him, counseled with him and his family, and married him to a sweet, stable young woman after he had been sober for over a year and was employed with a good company.

Paul had come by my study upon the completion of his year of sobriety to give me the poker chip marking that achievement. "I wanted you to have this," he said. "You've stuck by me." I knew I was only one of many who had supported him, but I was touched by his gesture.

Sadly, I had also rescued him from freezing, sleet-covered Williamsburg sidewalks in the middle of more winter nights than I want to remember. Recognizing me in unusual circumstances was not difficult for Paul.

"Wha—?" he mumbled as he partially succeeded in sitting with the help of a pillow I placed behind his back. I knew his question was going to be, "What are you doing here?" But before he finished that thought, he fell back onto the pillow and mumbled through hands covering his face, "Mother." It was a statement, not a question.

"Good thing you've got a 'muvver,'" I said.

"What?" he asked, puzzled. "Long story," I replied with a dismissive wave of my hand.

Nodding weakly while swinging his legs off the bed, Paul looked around as if he were seeing the room for the first time. "How'd you get in?"

I nodded toward the window I had left open to air out the foul-smelling bedroom. "I rang the doorbell and pounded on the door, but you didn't respond," I said. "Thanks for leaving that wooden box at the corner of the house so I could reach the window."

Paul lowered his head and shook it slowly. "Gotta get you a key," he said softly with a wry grin.

I handed him the cleanest washcloth I had been able to find in the bathroom. "Go wash your face. You stink."

Paul reluctantly climbed out of the rumpled bed and walked unsteadily toward the bathroom while I took a seat on the couch in the living room. When he finally emerged with wet hair and scrubbed face, Paul sat in a chair opposite me.

"Your mother was very worried," I said. "She's been calling all night and day. She was getting pretty frantic. Afraid you were dead."

"I know, I know," Paul replied sadly. "Mother's the only one in my family who cares anymore, and I hate to worry her."

"Mothers are something, aren't they?" I replied. "Just can't seem to stop loving." We talked for another thirty minutes before I finally asked, "You still in contact with your AA sponsor?" When Paul nodded, I said, "Go call him, and I'll leave."

I heard him talking to his sponsor on the kitchen phone setting up a meeting for later in the day. Standing as Paul returned, I said, "I'm going to see your mother now. She'll be glad you're still breathing. You need to give her a call."

His mother was quite ill from cancer and unable to leave the house because of weakness from the radiation and chemo treatments. Glancing back over my shoulder as I exited the door, I saw Paul give a slight nod of his head. "I will," he mumbled, barely audible.

I knew how much it hurt him to disappoint his mother. But that dreaded disease of alcohol addiction, which is now responsible for tens of thousands of deaths each year in the United States, still held Paul in its deathlike grip. It's interesting to me that the statistics on alcohol-related deaths say nothing about the tens of thousands of deaths of marriages, families, and careers.

I was deeply saddened as I walked to my car, wondering if Paul would ever be able to break free.

I was certain he would get no help from society at large. It was not surprising that one of the largest cuts in the recent Trump administration's tax cut was on beer, wine, and liquor.

By the way, have you ever noticed how any mention of drinking or drunkenness has become a favorite punchline? Giggling and outright laughter follow each mention of drinking, and especially references to overindulgence. Just listen to comedians—or the hosts and studio audiences of any talk show. From my experiences of dealing with the destructive power of alcoholism, the laughter sounds a lot like whistling past a graveyard.

Paul's mother preceded him in death by several years. Even though he had moved to another city, I tried to keep in touch with Paul, and occasionally he would call to let me know he was still living and having varying periods of sobriety—even working as an assistant to a Presbyterian minister for a while. Some years, I could not reach him because his phone number had changed.

So my heart was shattered and I could not hold back the tears when I received a call one winter morning as cold rain was falling outside my office window. Why was it always that kind of weather when I heard from Paul?

The call was from someone with whom Paul had grown up. His friend told me that Paul had been found dead on a street corner in downtown Richmond. No foul play was indicated. "Death by exposure," they said.

Paul's life summed up in three cold words: "death by exposure." They had no idea all he had been exposed to in his much-too-short life.

My secretary looked up, puzzled, as I hurried past her, unspeaking, with my head down on the way to the empty sanctuary, where I often went in search of peace.

Once again, I was able to find comfort. The wooden cross hanging on the wall behind the baptistery was dark now but still spoke of a love that is willing to die for its children, "[like a mother's love, which] always protects, always trusts, always hopes, always perseveres" (1 Cor 13:7).

As I bowed my head and began to pray, "Our Father," I was somewhat comforted that as he took his last breath on that freezing, dark street corner in Richmond, Virginia, Paul was still held in the arms of a mother's love.

# A Picture of My Insides

My forkful of fresh, crisp salad was halfway to my mouth when my cellphone rang. I had meant to turn it off. There are some things you just don't want interrupted. Eating is high on my list of uninterruptible things.

"Mr. Haywood," the excited voice of my doctor's assistant cried, "you are in AFib and the doctor wants you to go to the emergency room immediately."

"No, ma'am," I cried back, "I'm not in AFib. I'm in LongHorn."

Chuckling politely at my feeble attempt at humor, she continued, "How do you feel?"

"Kind of hungry," I said—a little too loudly, I realized, as diners around me were looking in my direction. Well, her panicky voice had interfered with my first full meal in a while.

Let me give you a little background to help you understand this scene.

Earlier that week, I had made a visit to my neurologist's assistant for the annual check of my CPAP machine. During the visit, the PA also checked my heart and called in her boss since she thought she detected a slight irregularity. I told her she was just supposed to check my machine and was meddling when she moved over into my personal space.

But her boss, the neurologist, did not agree with me and said something was going on and thought I needed an EKG. I told him that sounded too much like those suspicious organizations who only use alphabet names—NSA, FBI, IRS, SSA, CSI— just to name a few. They all make me nervous.

He chuckled, but without a modicum of sympathy or understanding as he sent orders for me to show up at the lab downstairs.

I finally got around to it late that Friday afternoon after a hectic, stressful week. I thought those kinds of weeks might disappear after I retired. I was terribly naive.

So three hours after the EKG, my wife and I stopped by LongHorn to use a gift certificate I had received for officiating at a recent wedding.

Listening to the phone conversation from across the table, Jean was becoming more and more agitated with me. "Let's just forget the food and go on to the hospital," she said, also a little too loudly.

"No!" I stubbornly persisted, a little out of my head with hunger.

My hunger resulted from the fact that I had been on a three-month nutrition and fitness program. Ended up the nutrition part meant I did not eat much—and hardly anything I actually enjoyed.

At the beginning of the program, they asked me, "Why do you want to do this?"

"Well," I replied, "I have a twelve-year-old grandson who loves to hike and fish, and I want to keep up with him for a few more years."

But now Brent had told me—twenty pounds later—that I was keeping up "real good" and should go back to eating. After three months you discover there are only so many ways to cook chicken so it doesn't taste like chicken. Red meat had become a fading memory of good times long past.

So that's why on this Friday evening we ended up at the LongHorn Steakhouse in our hometown of Williamsburg.

But in spite of what many people believe, I'm not a complete idiot. I called our waitress over and asked her to please box up all our food. "The steaks aren't ready yet," she said.

"I'll wait," I said. Jean threw me another dirty look, but I ignored it as I went to pay our bill and sit on the bench by the door to wait.

Suddenly remembering something, I ran back to our waitress and said, "Could you also put a place setting in with the steak? And plenty of napkins. I may be eating my steak in the hospital emergency room."

She looked at me incredulously—as if she had never heard of anyone eating a LongHorn steak in a hospital emergency room.

Just then, my phone rang again. This time it was my doctor, who had already left the office for the day. I heard her two sets of twins playing in the background as she told me she had been studying the report more thoroughly and did not feel it was necessary for me to go to the emergency room that night.

"Thank you so much," I cried. "You've just given me another reason to love you. Do you know how many Friday nights I've spent with parishioners in emergency rooms? It's an all-night affair—and I didn't bring a blanket or pillow to LongHorn."

She laughed and said goodbye, adding, "Just come see me early Monday morning, and we will plan a course of action."

On Monday an echocardiogram was ordered. "Thank you for not calling it by its alphabetical name," I said. A puzzled frown crossed her face briefly, but she let it pass. We had become good friends over the years, and she had given up long ago trying to make sense of everything I said.

But the prospect of that echocardiogram caused me some anxiety. No one had ever looked closely at my insides—especially my heart. Except, of course, for the Lord Jesus, and he did so with a lot of grace and love. I wasn't sure about these folks.

Turned out my heart was healthy, except for the AFib, which the cardiologist said was minor and could be controlled with medication. "It's very common," he added.

I haven't often enjoyed being called "common." Like most people, I like to be considered a little special. But when it concerns your health, I guess "common" can be a good thing.

All this started me thinking. For seventy-eight years I had been fortunate that it had been unnecessary for anyone to look carefully at my insides. Not even a chest x-ray. But the time seemed to have come when it was necessary. I didn't like it, but I did like the idea of hiking and fishing with my grandson for a few more years.

The anxiety over having my physical insides scrutinized stirred memories of those people over the years who have been equally or perhaps more anxious when it came to looking carefully at their spiritual insides. This became especially obvious each year during Lent when I would begin talking about examining ourselves in preparation for Easter.

"I don't want to look at my heart too closely," a man told me—the last of many who have said similar things over the years. "I already know too much about myself. Not sure I could handle any more poking through the garbage my heart has collected, Pastor."

But that's our only hope, isn't it? Just as my physical insides needed to be looked at if the problem was to be discovered, our soul is in the same need of having disease identified and then treated.

Take it from me. It's scary to have your insides examined closely. But God has already seen them—and loves us still. So have hope. There is grace enough for the most severe spiritual sickness. We don't deserve it or earn it. It can only be given freely, and we can only receive it: "In him we have redemption through his blood, the forgiveness of sins, in accordance with the riches of God's grace that he lavished on us" (Eph 1:7–8).

We may not like what our insides reveal. But if we are going to make it all the way to Mullinix, a careful examination is needed in order to make way for God to lavish his grace upon us.

That abundance of grace often leaves me breathless. It's also my only possibility of being made well.

# Epilogue: The End of the Story?

My lunch companion carefully placed his spoon beside the half-eaten bowl of Brunswick stew, leaned back in the creaking wooden chair, and asked with a mischievous twinkle in his eyes, "Jerry, what is a story?"

My very thin yet very tasty country ham biscuit—Mother would have considered these biscuits "fallen" and tossed them in the slop bucket for the hogs—was halfway to my mouth. My mouth remained open, but the biscuit never passed through the eager cavity as I placed it back on my plate, which also contained a half-full bowl of the famous Old Chickahominy House Brunswick stew.

Dr. Chevis Horne, longtime pastor of the First Baptist Church of Martinsville, was in Williamsburg, Virginia, to lead our church, just down the hill from the Chickahominy House on Jamestown Road, in a series of renewal services.

Chevis knew of my life-long love affair with stories. But he guessed correctly that it had been a long time since I had been asked to define *story*. A project in which he was involved had brought the question to his mind. Chevis was obviously amused at my stammering.

"Well," I said thoughtfully, "I'm not sure I can define *story*. I know a story has a beginning, a middle, and an end. And I think I know something about what each of those parts should contain. But that's not much of a definition."

With a coy smile still plastered across his amused face, Chevis interrupted. "Does a story always have an ending, Jerry?" He was really enjoying this.

"Maybe not," I conceded. "But I sure like it when it does."

Chuckling, Chevis picked up his spoon and dipped it into the still warm Brunswick stew.

I was confessing the truth about myself and probably a lot of other people. I do not like unfinished stories. For instance, I do not like to read books that trace generations of a family *ad infinitum*, sailing all the way from England to the New World and settling in my hometown of Mt. Gilead, North Carolina.

Each book in the series ends with the unfinished story of a generation and then resumes the story in the next volume, which may not be published for several months—or years. My inner voice calls out, "Finish the story already!" Sometimes, I confess, my outer voice shouts it aloud. In frustration I usually end reading with the family still floundering in the middle of the ocean. It's not my fault if the author left them there to drown, their journey unfinished.

Nor do I intentionally watch television programs that do not conclude the story at the end of the current episode. Worst of all are the cliffhangers that misguided writers and producers believe are certain to bring gullible viewers back for the next season.

It's sad to think that it must work because it's been going on for a long time. Probably "Who shot J.R.?" was the beginning of that whole sordid trend. If you don't know who J.R. is, ask your parents—or maybe your grandparents. I never showed up for the answer to that question nor to any of the other countless cliffhangers since.

My wife has trouble understanding why I mutter in frustration when a program we're watching unexpectedly flashes those dreaded words across the screen: "To be continued…" Jean shakes her head and frowns when I say, "Well, another hour wasted."

But I wouldn't expect anyone who has watched *General Hospital* and *Days of Our Lives* for decades without experiencing a satisfying ending to any of their myriad plots to understand my annoyance at such things. Even death is not an ending in those soaps, as Jean excitedly tells me about the latest "rising from the grave" of one of her favorite characters. I'm convinced there are more resurrections on those soaps than in the entire Bible.

I know all of this might sound terribly petty, but to be fair to myself, I think the primary reason I feel so strongly about the need for an ending in my entertainment is that unfinished stories are too much like real life. I want entertainment to give me a temporary *escape* from reality.

For instance, solutions to conflicts and problems are at best only temporary in this world. When counseling sessions with couples have ended and I watch them leave, I wonder how long it will be before they return. I know the story of their conflict isn't finished.

Folks sometimes ask me to help them find closure after a death or a terrible loss. Of course I offer what comfort I can. But I know their sorrow over the tragic death of a beautiful little child will never be over. There is no closure for that kind of grief. That story will never be finished on this earth.

Nor should it be. As one father cried out bitterly when I was attempting to help him and his wife deal with the loss of a young daughter, "I don't *want* to forget her!"

Stories are rarely ended in this world.

So back to the subject of one of my pet peeves—entertainment. From my perspective, for entertainment to be enjoyable and satisfying, it must provide a definitive ending—preferably a happy ending, a Hallmark ending.

Now, this desire for a decisive ending may sound a little strange to those who know me and are aware that I have chosen to live my life, as a Christian pastor, *in* and *out* of an unfinished story.

The work of grace that God has begun in me has not been completed—which is painfully obvious to those who know me. In fact, I never expect to be a finished product on this earth.

*Still Going to Mullinix*

I can easily identify with Paul when he confessed, "Not that I have already obtained all this, or have already arrived at my goal, but I press on to take hold of that for which Christ Jesus took hold of me" (Phil 3:12).

Paul certainly recognizes in many of his writings that God's grace has redeemed him. But he is also keenly aware that he has fallen short of reaching the full potential of the redeemed. Even more, there is the implication that Paul expects his earthly life's story to end unfinished—short of the goal of authentic Christlikeness. Short of reaching the metaphorical Mullinix. Pressing on, but not obtained.

I love the story that came out of the Crittenden household over in Deltaville, Virginia, while I was interim pastor at Zoar Baptist. The family was gathered for the Thanksgiving meal. Howard, the beloved husband and father and grandfather, had been given a wonderful reprieve when the doctor said, "No, you don't have a brain tumor." So he was grateful beyond words that his life had been given back to him—even more precious than before.

Bowing his head to say grace, Howard was overcome with a sense of giftedness and said thoughtfully, "How do I start?" He paused a few moments in an effort to gain control of his emotions before repeating, "How do I start?"

Thinking his grandfather was now seriously stuck, little grandson Alex whispered out of the corner of his mouth, "Papa, you start by saying, 'Dear God.'"

If, in the course of making our way through this world of faith and mystery—if somewhere along the way we have learned to say those words in deep submission, "Dear God"—we have joined our life's story to God's story of grace and promise, which is never quite finished in this life.

No, Chevis, not every story has an ending. But I've bet my last breath that this one does. Not in my time. Not in my place. But in God's time. In God's place.

Where, finally, "'God himself will be with them and be their God. He will wipe every tear from their eyes. There will be no more death or mourning or crying or pain, for the old order of things has passed away'" (Rev 21:3d–4).

That's an unfinished story I can live with *now* as I await God's ending *then*. In fact, I don't think I can live without it.

So the journey continues…

CPSIA information can be obtained
at www.ICGtesting.com
Printed in the USA
BVHW040117120721
611299BV00008B/18

9 781635 281439